Trinny&
Susannah

What your clothes say about you

How to look different, act different and feel different

Trinny & Susannah

What your clothes say about you

How to look different, act different and feel different

**Trinny Woodall and
Susannah Constantine**

Photography by Robin Matthews

WEIDENFELD & NICOLSON

TO OUR BELOVED MICHAEL FOSTER

First published in Great Britain in 2006
by Weidenfeld & Nicolson

By arrangement with the BBC
The BBC logo is a trade mark of the British Broadcasting Corporation and is used under licence.
BBC logo © BBC 1996
What Not to Wear logo © BBC 2002

Hair by Cristiano Basciu at Richard Ward Hair & Beauty,
162B Sloane St, Knightsbridge, London SW1X 9BS
Make-up by Charlotte Ribeyro
Styling by Zoe Lem
Additional research by Jessica Jones

A CIP catalogue record for this book
is available from the British Library.

ISBN 1 84188 265 8

Design director David Rowley
Editorial director Susan Haynes
Designed by Lippa Pearce
Edited by Jinny Johnson
Design assistance by Justin Hunt

Printed in Italy

Weidenfeld & Nicolson

The Orion Publishing Group Ltd
5 Upper St Martin's Lane
London WC2H 9EA
www.orionbooks.co.uk

Contents

Introduction

When we started out as amateur style-dilemma solvers, we created a foolproof way of dressing for women based not on the latest trends, but on body shape. In our last television series we realised that to create a long-term change in attitude to dressing, we had to go even further – we had to understand WHY women find it difficult to change, and what we could do to help them. We have listened and we have really heard the fears and anxieties that keep women stuck in a rut.

Like it or not, the way you appear says something about you. This is the first impression that others receive. Sometimes it is the only one. Are your clothes giving out a positive message? Do you even know what they are saying? People cannot look inside your head to see the confident, warm, creative, sexy, adventurous woman hiding beneath that frumpy, tired, boring or just plain scary exterior. If you met a friend for dinner and she hadn't bothered to get out of her tracksuit, brush her hair or put on any make-up it may be that she was feeling down in the dumps and tired, but you might equally suspect that she just didn't think that you were worth the effort. To take this analogy further, it would be just plain rude to turn up to your cousin's wedding wearing your work suit. Presenting yourself appropriately and with élan is a gift you give to others, in much the same way that you might give them flowers. And we know you wouldn't dream of presenting a friend with a bouquet of wilting blooms.

You don't have to have the physique of a super model to look great. Real style is the ability to reflect all the positive aspects of who you truly are through how you dress and present yourself. This book is not about how to dress like 'Trinny and Susannah', it is about dressing to express *yourself*. When your outside reflects your inside you feel at ease. Others feel comfortable and proud to be with you, and so confidence grows.

Most of our audience know the rules of dressing by now – which shapes and lengths suit you, which colours are complementary and how to dress for certain occasions. What the last series really brought home to us was just how many of you are bogged down and deeply unhappy about your appearance. Speaking to all the women we met during the last series we were amazed at the personal issues that were unlocked through talking about what you wear. It may be that age or circumstances have crept in, sapped your confidence and overtaken your life. It may be fear. It may be laziness. It may be putting everyone and everything before yourself. What all the women we encountered had in common was that they did not initially have the courage to change – to feel good about themselves again.

What your clothes say about you takes you on a journey of self-discovery. You can expect to identify with many of the chapters. We have listened to women and observed how they have expressed themselves to us – the reasons, both stated and internalised, that have brought them to their present state. Women's own words are important and we have used these to get at the crux of each problem. We have met each of these states of mind again and again and we understand how important clothes and presentation are in initiating change. Tracy, who appeared in one of our television shows, summed it up most eloquently – 'If only I could look good – maybe I could feel good.'

Recognising yourself, or elements of yourself, is the first step in identifying possibilities for change. Now, we can hear you thinking: 'Well that may be true for the women who appear on Trinny and Susannah's TV show, but I'm not one of them'. Ho, ho, think again! The reason we can so readily recognise the issues we describe in this book is that, between the two of us, we have at some time in our lives manifested *all* of them ourselves. Trinny has at various times found herself strongly identifying with several of the chapters. When Trinny was younger she used to work in the city, in an office with one other woman and thirty men. Feeling less than the guys and not wanting to be singled out as a woman she would do anything to fit in. So she took to wearing a man's suit every day and swearing a lot. With hindsight she can see that she was trying to compete in a man's world on men's terms and now realises that she could never win playing that game. In another phase of her life Trinny attached undue importance to the possession of certain designer labels. The arrival of her pay cheque would see her running to her favourite stores for the thrill of a new purchase, which inevitably would cost more than her wages. The result was debt, fear, a feeling of emptiness and being unable to really enjoy the beautiful garment she had bought.

Looking back through the years Trinny relates to so many small aspects of each woman in this book that it makes her simultaneously cringe and laugh out loud. Worst of all was her five years of wearing excessive fake tan. She would look in the mirror and worry that she looked pale. What began as a small addiction eventually developed into a total compulsion to apply the bronzer every day. Fuelled by a fear of becoming blotchy she gradually turned bright orange! Trinny just couldn't see it – but everyone else could.

Susannah, on the other hand, recalls when a photo of her appeared in the press wearing a far-too-short skirt with laddered tights and a plunging neckline. She received a curt letter from her grandmother saying: 'I have no need to tell you what you look like... a cheap tart.' Susannah was mortified. And the times when, through shyness and wanting her clothes to do the talking, her 'baby doll' look was a favourite for big events – billowing chiffon and overdone hair coupled with too much make-up made everyone think she'd come in fancy dress.

With Susannah's first baby came a realisation that nothing would stay clean for more than five minutes so what was the point of wearing anything decent? The result was a figure constantly shrouded in hoodies, man-cut Levis and loafers, a complete eradication of her sexuality, and finally a few sharp words from Trinny. You may not identify with *everything* that is said about every character in this book, but if you keep an open mind and look for the similarities, rather than the differences, we guarantee that you will find aspects of yourself in many of the women we describe.

Next it is time to face up to how others see you. We have taken quotes directly from those closest to the many women who have appeared on our shows and they are featured on the 'How others see you' spreads. It can be quite shocking to hear what people won't tell you to your face. Frankly, it really hits home.

Turning the page you will be confronted with an extreme example of how you really look. It's rock-bottom time. We are ruthless in assessing where you have got to – and what your clothes are saying about you.

Once the denial is swept away, our remedy begins. The following pages will encourage you to persevere. The remedy itself is not about a specific outfit, but more how a total change in attitude to your old look is required. We have included a section of *Life tips,* which we don't cover in our television series, at the end of each chapter. These are action points for reassessing and rediscovering the joy in your life. It's time to do the best for yourself. We have lots of suggestions.

What your clothes say about you is about recognising that we all communicate things about ourselves through how we dress. It will show you how to retune your appearance so that you can tell the world who you want to be. We will help you to give a positive message, which is still delivered in your own unique voice. We want you to feel attractive, happy and proud to be you. When you look different you will act different, and when you act different you will feel different.

More than any other book, this is going to be like having us by your side. We really will feel like your ally and confidante because we've been there, so we speak from the heart.

1

'What's the making an anymore?'

point in
effort

**'YOUR LIFE IS *NOT* OVER YET,
SO DON'T ACT LIKE IT IS'**
TRINNY AND SUSANNAH

What I say...

Comfort is the name of the game. I like to feel well covered up.

I don't need smart clothes, I don't go out that much.

This big coat keeps me warm.

I hardly ever dry-clean my clothes.

My underwear is all mismatched and stretched.

Most of my clothes are black.

My make-up is all broken and years old.

Everything in my flat is piled up and a bit grubby.

This big shoulder bag is bulging full and I carry other things I need in plastic shopping bags.

My favourite shoes are broken down and scuffed.

What I really feel inside...

I don't feel comfortable showing my body.

There's nobody in my life to dress up for any more.

This shapeless coat protects me from the world. I've had my fair share of knock downs, I don't want to risk more.

Are they really that dirty?

I'm not sexy. If I put on nice underwear I might ultimately feel disappointment.

Nobody really sees me anyway. I may as well be invisible.

My face is broken and years old.

I don't really want people coming round to visit me at home.

All the things that I have to do every day are a real burden to me.

Life is a hard road to travel.

How you look

When did you last look in the mirror, hmm? Or do you even have a mirror? Probably not. Caught sight of your reflection in a polished shop window recently? Oh God, no, you haven't been near the high street on a shop-up for years now, have you?

Your appearance is heartbreakingly lacking in care. We want to weep when we look at you. The greatest sadness is, however, that you have achieved what you set out to achieve with flying colours. Your desire to blend into nothing has turned you into a ghost-like figure that no-one notices – not even enough to feel sorry for you. The only reason that we can see you is because our experienced eyes find it hard not to rest on outfits that are so pitiful.

Sweetheart, to be honest, you look like a bag lady. Your clothes are so worn they seem ingrained with grime, rigid with dirt and alive with bacteria. Those big, baggy, heavy-knit sweaters and over-sized jackets may be warm, may even aid you in your bid to evaporate into the atmosphere, but they've swallowed you up so effectively that you are unable to find the person you once were. Your appearance has wiped you from the face of the earth. Even your shoes represent a life dedicated to giving up. They are androgynous loafers or tired trainers. The soles are worn, the heels sloping. The upside is that

they are perfectly in tune with the plastic bag you use as a handbag. The downside is that these 'accessories' have the same feeling of despondency as your clothes.

And the hair, oh dear, the hair. This has a year-round snowy peak above the tresses that cling to the colour from your bi-annual dyeing session. If you do make the effort with make-up, you just add to what's left from the day before.

Nothing you do enhances your looks; the overall impression you give is one of extreme visual tiredness.

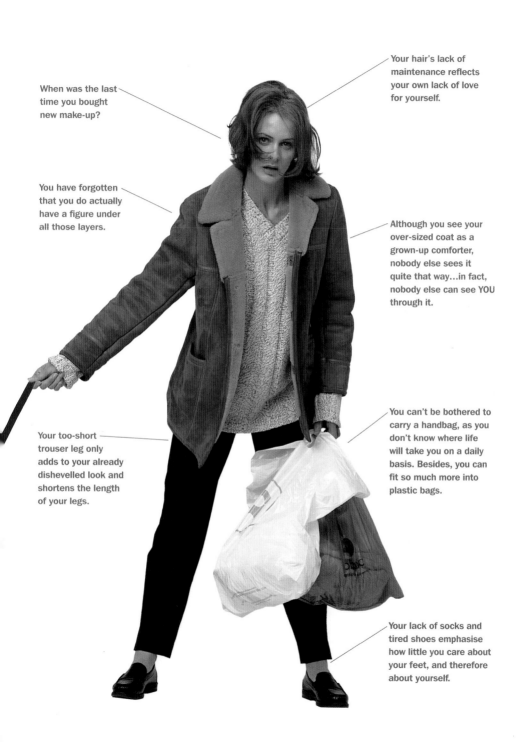

Your hair's lack of maintenance reflects your own lack of love for yourself.

When was the last time you bought new make-up?

You have forgotten that you do actually have a figure under all those layers.

Although you see your over-sized coat as a grown-up comforter, nobody else sees it quite that way...in fact, nobody else can see YOU through it.

You can't be bothered to carry a handbag, as you don't know where life will take you on a daily basis. Besides, you can fit so much more into plastic bags.

Your too-short trouser leg only adds to your already dishevelled look and shortens the length of your legs.

Your lack of socks and tired shoes emphasise how little you care about your feet, and therefore about yourself.

How others see you

'She hates herself. She's not interested in her life' – mum

'Her dress sense is very easy to describe, it's basically cover everything up, all in one, black from head to toe' – friend

'It's almost like she hasn't bothered getting dressed' – work colleague

'We've kind of given up asking her out because she never wants to come' – friend

'It's scary to think I might end up like that' – daughter

'Me and my sister walk about 20 paces behind her in the street' – son

'It's as if she's just disappeared into herself' – friend

'She used to be so stylish and fashionable, I think she's lost her confidence' – daughter

Dear Friend

It seems you don't have a care in the world – about yourself. In fact, you don't give a damn about yourself. Your life has fallen into a deep crevasse and you are unable to hoist yourself out. What was it that sent you off into the sunset of stagnation? Could it have been the kids leaving home, menopause, bolshy teenagers, divorce? Perhaps you have been suffering from a bout of mild depression or maybe you've just been working too damn hard? We women have so much piled upon us that it's hardly surprising some of us slowly slide away from stress, upset and advancing years into a muddy puddle of decline. Isn't it easier to surrender one's being to oblivion than constantly to fight against a future you have no control over? Well, actually NO, it isn't. Goddammit, girl. We cannot let this happen to you. We will not allow you to let yourself go to the point where you believe your life, as you knew it, is over for good.

We can tell how you feel on the inside by the way you dress. Your façade is a direct reflection of your neglected interior. It may come as a surprise, however, that the low opinion you have of yourself is not shared by those around you. You are your own worst enemy. It's you that is responsible for this dereliction, and surrounding circumstances are only contributors to your lack of self-esteem.

The thing is, what is going to lift you out of this rut? The most obvious catalyst for change is the basic desire to do so. But do you have the courage to change? Ask yourself: do you want to try a new life? Do you want to like yourself again and feel that you ARE worth your weight in gold? This may seem an impossible task from where you stand today.

Some people would say that a course of anti-depressants or time on the psychotherapist's couch is the only answer. Both these routes have been tried and tested and are known to work extremely well. While we can't prescribe drugs and are not qualified to take you on a psychological journey back to your childhood, we are able to offer some good, practical, woman-to-woman advice that we know works.

Think back to the last time you felt good about yourself physically. What was different then? Okay, your body may have given in to gravity and the wrinkles on your face may have been around the world a couple of times, but it's not like you went to bed a teenager and woke up an OAP. Age has crept up slowly and tapped you on the shoulder. If you hadn't decided that there was no point in making an effort, you would still be the fabulous you. Nothing has altered your personality. Your character has taken years to build – much longer than the time it has taken for you to become the person you feel you are now. That fun-loving woman is still in you. We just have to rediscover her.

Please trust us when we say that clothes and grooming can dramatically change the way you feel.

The remedy

Clothes have stopped being fun for you long ago.
They have become a necessity and no more. It's time to
re-evaluate your wardrobe and only keep the items that
you really wear all the time. You will feel that less of your
past is hanging around in a murky corner. Go through
your wardrobe. Put your clothes into the following piles:

DRY-CLEANING

Even if something just smells of a late night and
has no visible stains, it needs to be dry-cleaned.
Your clothes will feel new and the cost of dry-
cleaning is much less than buying it again.

MENDING

Look for broken zips, falling-down hems, clothes
that are too large. Find a friendly seamstress
and get them fixed.

TOO OLD

Clothes that have been in your wardrobe for
too many years without being worn need to go.
You will have more than most other people.
Sentimentality, or the hope of a diet working,
are not reasons to let redundant items take up
valuable space. THROW THEM OUT NOW.

TOO SMALL

It's far better to let go of items that have
not fitted you for a number of years than cling
onto the hope that your size will change. Let
them go now. If you do lose weight, you won't
want to wear them anyway.

COLOUR AND SHAPE

Once you have created this space in your
wardrobe – either go shopping or swapping.
First stop: buy a new coat. This will be an item
that will show off your figure, yet hide the
middle-age spread. Don't choose black. You
need colour in your life. Really try to lighten up
the tone of your wardrobe. Most women who
have given up tend to have a very dark-coloured
wardrobe. Work out which colours suit you (see
What you wear can change your life) and start to
build up with the basics. Look carefully at the
SHAPE of your clothes – are your waistbands
too high, your tops too low, your hems betraying
ageing knees? Can your arms take those puff
sleeves, your legs those cropped trousers?

Wearing a fitted coat or jacket is a great way to look smart and feel not past it. If you don't know which skirt length is best for you, opt for trousers instead.

A long scarf with the colour of the bag in it lifts the outfit out of 'beigedom'.

Show that you have respect for yourself and carry a decent handbag.

A flared or wide-legged trouser is just as practical as a tapered jean. Don't be frightened of something you may consider too modern.

You can't let this new look down by wearing anything other than a pair of flattering heels. Forget your heavy black flatties.

Finishing touches

We are pretty certain that any form of grooming disappeared with your self-respect quite a few years ago. There is no more effective way to plummet your self-esteem than feeling unkempt and looking grubby. We believe that cleanliness is the route to godliness.

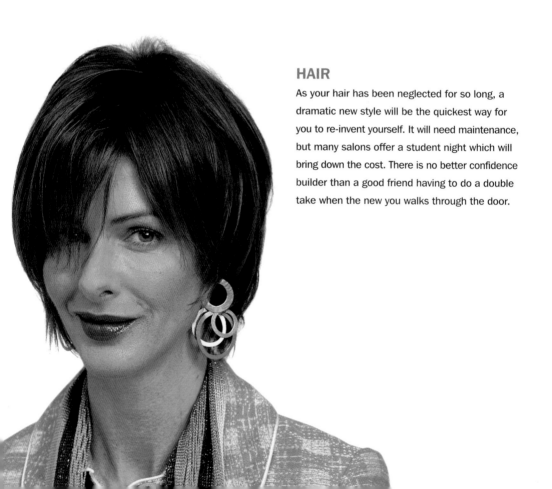

HAIR

As your hair has been neglected for so long, a dramatic new style will be the quickest way for you to re-invent yourself. It will need maintenance, but many salons offer a student night which will bring down the cost. There is no better confidence builder than a good friend having to do a double take when the new you walks through the door.

COSMETICS

Since you last addressed your skin care routine, we guarantee that your face has changed…if indeed you still maintain any kind of skin care routine. Now is the time to catch up before it is too late. You need to scrub off those years of neglect. Start with an exfoliator. Your skin needs waking up. Each morning take three minutes to scrub your face, gently around the eyes, but quite firmly elsewhere, and use a flannel to wash off the product. Follow with a good moisturiser. You will be left with glowing, younger-looking skin.

SCARF

Guess what? As well as keeping your neck warm, a scarf is an accessory. Scarves are a great, inexpensive way to pull your look together, adding colour and sparkle. Try to acquire a good collection of scarves in all the colours of your palette. Wearing a scarf that picks out one of the colours from your top, jacket or handbag completes any outfit with élan. Include some with sequins, or in shimmery silk and acetate knits as well as the practical woolly variety.

SHOES

Your shoes or boots haven't seen any polish since they were bought. You probably only wear two pairs of the many you have hidden in your wardrobe. Throw out every single tired-looking pair. Once you have banished the trainers and the scuffed chunky heels, you'll see that your legs and ankles do have a good shape and benefit from a lighter style of shoe (that isn't black, either).

BAG

You will probably always want to carry your life around with you, so don't go for small. Find something that will hold the kitchen sink, just do it with a bit more style. Choose a bright clashing colour like orange – it will really give you a kick.

MAKE-UP

You need to throw out all your make-up. We know you haven't bought anything new for years, and cosmetics do have a sell-by date. The colours you have are probably all wrong for you anyway. Remember the key basics: if you have a very lined skin, avoid powder and go for a moisturising foundation instead. If your lips are thin: opt for a lip gloss rather than a lipstick.

Life tips

Look around your home. Is it tired, cluttered and just a little bit dirty? Take a day to go round your house to touch all of your possessions and choose to have them in your life. Then get rid of everything that is not chosen. Now you'll be living in a home where everything feels loved and in its place. If you can manage it, hire a cleaner, if only for a couple of hours a week. Even if you are a cleaner yourself, sometimes you need help.

It's all about being okay with yourself and rediscovering your life. Your kids have left home, you might be divorced. You might be experiencing menopause or maybe you have suffered from a period of mild depression. Or maybe you've just been working too hard. You feel that there's not much to get out of bed for except for the same old routine, that you're not really involved in your own life, that you're just a spare part. You may feel lonely, yet you're not desperate to make new friends. Everything has fallen into a rut. You've done your best for your kids, your husband, your boss...now do the same for yourself.

Even if you don't feel bright and breezy, act as if you do. A smile is the best instant facelift. Try smiling at ten strangers a day and you will be amazed at the response – don't overdo it though or they might come after you with a net.

Indulge in a spa day with a facial and massage. You'll feel rejuvenated afterwards, walk taller and glow from within.

Make a date with yourself once a week and go to the cinema, a gallery, a play, a restaurant. Each week do something different that you've always wanted to do. Just enjoy your own company.

Taking this a step further, go on holiday in your own town. Book into a hotel for a long weekend, but don't tell anyone where you're going. Then do all the things that you would do on holiday – museums, tourist attractions, long walks. Rediscover the place where you live. Maybe you'll fall in love with it all over again.

When? Alone, on your
self-indulgent holiday.

Why? After trying out
this glamorous look on
strangers, you'll return
home a confident, new
woman.

Tracy had the courage to redisc

Remember

 Dress to feel attractive to yourself. Others will notice and feel attracted to you too.

* Polish and repair your shoes and boots and use shoe-trees to keep their shape. Shoes take lots of wear and tear and can start to look tired very quickly.

* Even if your clothes don't have obvious stains they probably smell. Dry-clean all your clothes regularly, especially coats and sweaters.

* Chuck out those clothes that looked great when you were younger but you no longer wear. They're only making you depressed every time you look at them.

* Wearing sexy underwear makes you feel, and act, sexy. Nobody can see it but they can tell!

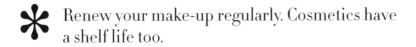 Choose different handbags for different occasions. Changing the contents regularly from one bag to another will make you realise how much unnecessary junk you're carting around with you. Only carry what you absolutely need.

Renew your make-up regularly. Cosmetics have a shelf life too.

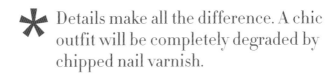 Details make all the difference. A chic outfit will be completely degraded by chipped nail varnish.

When you're out in the street, check your posture in a shop window. Are you still walking tall or have you slipped back into that old slouch?

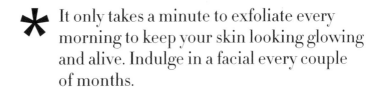 It only takes a minute to exfoliate every morning to keep your skin looking glowing and alive. Indulge in a facial every couple of months.

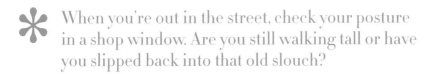

2

'I have an i
to uphold'

mage

'BUT YOU HAVE A PERSONALITY
TOO, DON'T YOU?'

TRINNY AND SUSANNAH

What I say...

Black works with everything.

I have to maintain the corporate image.

Everyone would like to look glamorous all the time,
but it's not reality.

I don't think I could wear fishnet tights.

This is my best suit, I wear it everywhere.

I'm a strong, independent woman.

I refuse to throw away my white cotton knickers –
they're so innocent, they haven't done anybody any harm.

Jewellery makes me rattle when I run.

The aim is to blend in.

What I really feel inside...

Better safe than sorry.

I prefer it to my self-image.

My reality is humdrum.

Someone might look at my legs and get the wrong idea.

Everywhere in my world is work, work, work, the wine bar and work.

It's tough working in a man's world so I act tough in order to get by.

Sex is not a big consideration for me. Practicality is far more important. I'm prim and proper, through and through.

I'm always running. Busy, busy, busy!

I have to protect myself from seeming to be a threat to my colleagues.

How you look

We know that your job plays a huge part in your life. So much so that it has infiltrated the very essence of who you are. You may not be aware of this, but corporate existence has had a profound effect on your wardrobe.

You dress like an office worker from one full moon to the next. Office clothes have snuck into your weekends and evenings. Time out has taken on a distinctly be-suited air, as souvenirs from your desk stalk your every outing.

It's absolutely fine for a woman to wear a suit. There are times and places when a suit, be it of skirt or trouser persuasion, is more…well, more suitable.

Sensible shoes in navy or black, too, have their place in the world. Just don't ever let it be at our place if you get invited for a recreational affair.

You see, this is the problem with your dress sense. It seems you find it hard to differentiate between work and play. In the same way as some people bring their job woes into the home and are incapable of switching off, you find it impossible to leave your proverbial briefcase at the office. Your pinstripe jacket will often get taken to the cinema or out for dinner. Likewise your hefty kitchen-sink bag will accompany your one and only black tie outfit.

Your work clothes are fortunate because they have seen more of life than any other garments we know. Let's face it, how many other black polyester-mix, single-breasted skirt suits do YOU know going to the ballet or pub? How many other 30 denier tights have YOU come across lucky enough to be sported on a hot summer's day at a picnic in the park?

When you are actually at work you leap feet first into corporate conformity. Not one iota of individuality ruffles your plain, colourless, buttoned-up surface. Are you hoping to be promoted to cardboard cut-out in chief?

The bottom line, baby, is that we see a woman who wears her job on her sleeve – quite literally. Black, navy, grey and white dominate your life right down to your underwear. The styles and shapes hanging in that closet of yours are pitifully limited. What does it contain? A couple of suits, jeans, sweats, trainers and the odd sparkly top that will invariably get swamped by grey flannel and bastardised by a pair of your ghastly square-toed, cubed heel, clumpy shoes.

Ask yourself: 'How long have I had this hairstyle?' It stopped flattering you a long time ago.

The combination of a white shirt with a black suit makes you look like you're wearing a uniform. You are not a number, you are a free woman.

Black is a colour that suits only 30% of the population, maybe 50% if they all wear make-up. Unless a black suit is exquisitely cut, there's no faster way to look drab.

Tights this thick might never ladder, but are they doing anything for the shape of your leg?

The only merit to this shapeless old bag is its practicality. It adds zero to your outfit.

How others see you

'**Bland!**' – **boyfriend**

'The suits she buys are cheap and I think they're quite manly looking' – friend

'**Practicality rules!**' – colleague

'Dull!' – sister

'She's a very creative, expressive person...it doesn't come across in how she dresses' – brother-in-law

'Scruffy!' – male friend

'I've known her for six years. To date I've *never* seen her leg' – male friend

'She is *determined* to dress depressed' – Susannah

Dear Friend

Dress in a dull way and you'll spread the rumour that you are a dull person. You might well be able to drink the boys under the snooker table, but wouldn't it be nicer to snog them when you got down there.

We think that your lack of confidence in the style stakes actually prevents you from going out sometimes. It's fine when you are in a position to demonstrate your intelligence, but when it comes to showing off your femininity you fall to pieces. You simply haven't got a clue. Some of you may even be a little snobby towards anyone with a touch of glamour. You assume that women who take time to lip gloss their mouths or paint their toenails are perhaps shallow or even dim.

We also know how important it is for you to look like you are in control, but after six pints will your power suit be enough to keep you standing? A tipsy girl in a cute little dress will be looked after, while a lass with a severe haircut and no accessories will have her vulnerability dismissed because she looks like a lady who can vomit into her briefcase without any assistance at all.

It's a shame, because you are a lovely person with a very soft side. But wearing all this monochrome armour could be preventing you from striking up all manner of relationships, including a long-lasting love one.

Well, we've got news for you: the smarter women are the ones who wield their sexuality like a sabre on the battlefields of big business. They are the ones who beguile their opponents into wanting to offer the world – just for another smile. This said, lightening up on the colour front and softening the fabrics of your clothes isn't taken on just as ammunition. Dressing up is, as you will discover, immense fun. You can do it on your own or with your girlfriends. You'll get excited, knowing you are going to look great in your killer heels and halter-neck top at tomorrow night's party. Your hangover won't be so bad because you will not have drunk so much to compensate for your drab clothes.

Your style has been box-filed into boardroom banality for far too long. It's time to break free from the constrained clothing that has been so influenced by your job. We appreciate that this is a big scary move, especially at work. You will probably be terrified that the boys in the office will snigger at you, but honey, do you really presume that just because you are wearing a burgundy skirt and cerise fine-knit sweater that the quality of your work is going to plummet and result in a good sacking or demotion? Of course not. You are exactly the same person, even when your legs and a touch of cleavage are on show. You must have more confidence in your brain and complement it with a touch of sex appeal.

We are sure you want to add a bit of va-voom to your existence, but you are frightened to go there in case you will be rejected. Well, you probably would be, dressing the way you do today. Take our advice and cross the threshold of corporate/ritzy environments, and the world (not only the one with a desk and photocopier) will be yours to be accepted in and own. Off you go now. Shoo!

The remedy

More than any woman in this book, you have retreated into wearing a uniform and that's what we've got to get rid of. But in order to have the confidence to get into a more individual style you first of all need to rearrange your clothes.

WARDROBE

Look at the number of duplicates you have. How many black trousers, white shirts, beige suits, grey cardigans and black shoes? Unless any of these are beautifully cut and show off your figure to perfection, get rid of them. Be ruthless. It's the only way you'll succeed in changing.

SHOPPING

You've probably gone to the same shops over and again, where you've bought the same garments over and again. It's time to reassess how you buy your clothes. Head to a shop (Zara, for example) which offers stylish work and casual wear. If you are choosing a suit, go for one that gives you a waist and has a bit of interest in the fabric – a pin stripe, for example.

You also need to learn the concept of separates, so buy a skirt and a jacket which complement each other, rather than match. Choose a patterned jacket, pick a colour in that jacket and then find a skirt in that colour. If you're pear shaped, choose the darkest colour from the pattern for your skirt; if you're top heavy, choose one of the lighter colours.

COLOUR

Get out of the black. You think it goes with everything. In fact, it hardly goes with anything at all. Unless it's an exquisite piece it generally looks hard and cheap. What's more, if you look at all the blacks in your wardrobe you'll find that they're not one colour but a variety of shades ranging from purple to brown tints. Worn together they just look a mismatched mess. Once you've established your colour palette (there's great guidance on this in our previous book *What you wear can change your life*) and understood the concept of separates, you can endlessly supplement your outfits with different tops and accessories, all of which will work together.

PATTERN AND TEXTURE

Big blocks of plain colour can soon become wearing on the eye. Try breaking up your look by combining patterns (a pinstripe suit with a floral shirt, for example) and textures (a fitted tweed skirt with a fitted silk shirt always looks great).

Allowing a pretty colour or print to peek through will really lift your whole look from conservative to sophisticated.

Find tailoring to suit your shape. Boxy shapeless suits do not cover up myriad body types, they just make them all look the same – boxy and shapeless.

You don't have to scream into the office dressed from head to toe in vermillion and lime green. Keep a corporate air with a softer grey pinstripe rather than hard black.

Trousers are practical, but they don't have to be manly. Flat-fronted trousers flatter most midriffs and wider, longer leg lengths are much more elegant than short, ankle-cropping pegs. Please also try to wear a skirt or dress, even if only once a week.

A work bag need not look like a portable filing cabinet.

Finishing touches

Your outlook on life had become truly workmanlike. 'Practical and unadorned' sums it up perfectly. Fripperies like jewellery and handbags just didn't figure in your landscape. What's missing are the personal touches that define your individuality.

JEWELLERY

Jewellery is not just an early warning system to let them know you're coming as you run down the corridors from meeting to meeting. It will lift you and, dare we say it, add your own personality to everything you wear. Choose different jewellery for different outfits rather than wearing that little heart on a chain every day of your life. NB: a Swatch watch is not jewellery.

TIGHTS

If your legs are one of your assets, why leave them off the balance sheet? Show them to best advantage with a great pair of fishnets. In the colder months, a skirt suit needs leg apparel, but those thick, one-colour tights make your outfit look decidedly dowdy. Wearing patterned or fishnet tights will transform you from a frumpy Miss Marple into a sexy Miss Moneypenny.

PAINTING YOUR TOENAILS

Small things can have a big impact. You might feel that peep-toe shoes or sandals are not businesslike, but a good pedicure and nail varnish will give you a beautifully finished look. Much smarter than a scuffed black toe cap. It's easier to DIY than a fingernail job too, and less easy for people to spot the little mistakes. Just remember to touch up any chips and completely remove and refresh the nail varnish once a fortnight.

SHOES

Chunky and black does not equal comfortable and versatile. Look for a shoe with a supportive heel but, for goodness sake, a bit of elegance in the toe area. Once again, black is not always the most useful colour for accessories. Variations on dark brown, tan, plum, rust and olive green are all far more stylish and complementary.

BAGS

Yes, you have a job, so you need a big bag, but please find one with a bit of shape and try not to overstuff it. You'll only ruin the line of the bag and trash all the things inside. Empty your bag each night when you get home, chuck out or file anything that you don't need to carry and repack your bag. This will take two minutes. Downsize some of the contents as well. Do you *really* need that gigantic planner? You can fit all the information you want onto a Blackberry instead.

WORK TO PLAY

There's nothing more boring for your friends than seeing you turn up every evening in that same old suit you've been wearing all day. It will make you feel tired and it will make them feel like you don't think they're worth the effort. The solution here is to carry a few things in your bag that will transform your daywear into a night-time look. These need only be small and lightweight, for example: earrings, a pair of fishnet tights, scent, a more dramatic lipstick, an embroidered camisole to replace the work shirt, and a pair of sparkly heels to lift your spirits. Leave the big bag in the cloakroom and top off your outfit with a gorgeous little evening purse.

LIP GLOSS

We're guessing that you usually wear nothing on your lips or else a harsh matt lipstick. Either way, a soft gloss will make a subtle, yet remarkable change for you. Other people will notice, but they won't twig what you've done. Try saying the following to your mirror: 'It is my pleasure to present this report to the board', first with bare lips, then wearing your matt lipstick, and finally, with a luscious lip gloss. See the difference?

HAIR

Take the time to blow-dry and style your hair, perhaps on Sunday night? Then at least it will look great until Tuesday. If you find that you don't have time to deal with your hair anymore by Wednesday and you feel that you simply must scrape it back into that old ponytail, use some hairclips or flowers that will complement your outfit. Make sure that you brush your hair before you pull it back, otherwise you'll just end up with the 'rat's nest' look. Even a humble ponytail needs to be styled.

Life tips

We know that you're competing in what is, after all, a man's world of work. You feel that it might be inappropriate, even unprofessional, to draw attention to your femininity. Well, as the men would put it – bollocks! They knew you were a woman when they hired you and your feminine personality attributes are probably part of what makes you excel at your job. Looking great can only enhance your career prospects.

Every morning, repeat after us: 'I am a complete woman with a rich, rewarding life. I am good enough exactly as I am.' Doing this will make you totally cringe at first, but persevere. Stick this message on your mirror, on the fridge, in your car and just keep saying it until you believe it.

Take your break – every day. Get out of that office to walk or meditate in the park, read a book, window shop, go to a yoga class...anything that's not work! Lunch al-desko is no longer acceptable.

Wear something different every single day for a week. Vary your colours as well as your outfits. Count how many compliments you receive during that week.

Close the office door at six and leave your work there. Okay, you do have to work late sometimes but unless you're an A & E surgeon or a fire-fighter (and even they have lives too) there is NO EXCUSE for staying after hours every night.

Enrol in an evening class one night a week. Make sure that it's something completely frivolous and fun (ahem – advanced computer engineering is not allowed). This will also give you a rock-solid excuse for leaving work on time, at least once a week.

Make your work space into your own private world. Flowers and family photos on your desk will cheer up your day and remind you that you do have a wonderful life outside these walls.

Ditch the watch. It's the weekend – who cares what time it is? If you are wearing your watch in bed you need to see a therapist.

When? Relaxing at the weekend.

Why? You can't even *think* about work in these clothes.

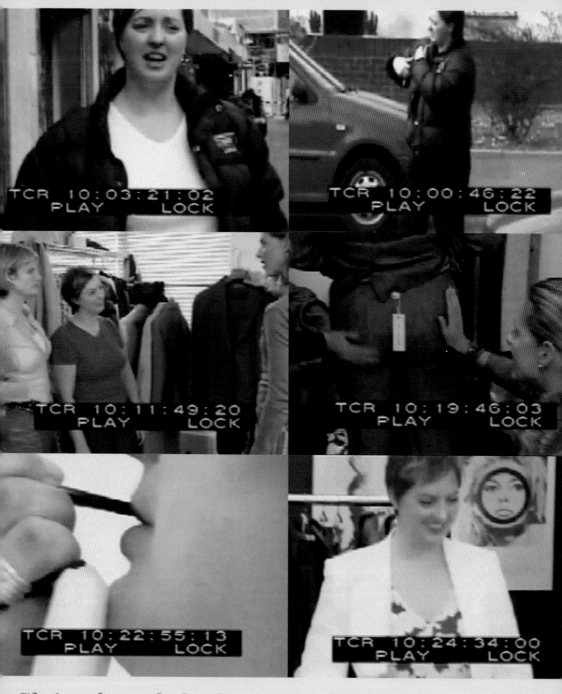

TCR 10:03:21:02 PLAY LOCK

TCR 10:00:46:22 PLAY LOCK

TCR 10:11:49:20 PLAY LOCK

TCR 10:19:46:03 PLAY LOCK

TCR 10:22:55:13 PLAY LOCK

TCR 10:24:34:00 PLAY LOCK

Claire found she had real flair and creativity.

TCR 10:06:09:12 PLAY LOCK

TCR 10:05:33:17 PLAY LOCK

TCR 10:19:10:11 PLAY LOCK

TCR 10:21:40:16 PLAY LOCK

TCR 10:27:45:03 PLAY LOCK

TCR 10:22:58:22 PLAY LOCK

Now she dresses to impress. So can you...

Remember

Be noticed – you are a woman. Believe it or not, that may be one of your great assets and not a hindrance to your career at all. Don't be afraid to show your femininity.

Spend some time finding out which colours suit you. Put all your clothes into colour piles: reds, blues, pinks, greens – even blacks and whites (include cream and ecru). In good daylight hold each item up to your face and see how it looks. Does it make you seem alive and sparkling, or does it bring out the inner corpse?

You will now know which are your basic good blues, reds, greens, whites, etc. Next learn how to combine these with complementary colours. A good shortcut is to look at the combinations in garments by designers who really understand colour, such as Missoni.

Get a new hairstyle every six to nine months. It may feel like a risk, but your hair will always grow back.

Black accessories are not the most useful. Look for muted browns, plums and greens which will work with most colours. You don't have to match your bag to your shoes.

Don't take your work home with you. Bring your home to work instead. Fill your office with personal touches, photographs and flowers, to make it into your own world.

Put together a quick-change kit to keep at the office in case of last-minute social invitations.

Beware of falling back into the duplication rut. Are you buying the same thing over and over again? Check out some different shops for a fresh overview of fashions.

Take a look at your wardrobe. Make sure that you can clearly define which outfits are casual, smart casual, evening and work. Try to avoid wearing bits of your work clothes, for example, your suit jacket, at the weekend. Forget about the office until Monday.

'My kids ar there's no t

e my life,
ime for me'

'IS *THAT* WHY YOU LOOK
SO BLAND?'

TRINNY AND SUSANNAH

What I say...

My children always come first.

At work, he's surrounded by smart, sophisticated women.

I don't seem to find the time to put on make-up in the morning.

Most of my money goes on the children.

I'm destined to wear vomit-proof, baby-proof, stretch-proof...

A lot of my friends, because they haven't got kids, have got beautiful, slim, size 8 figures.

A lot of my conversations are baby-related.

I am very capable as a mother and as a wife.

The last time someone told me I looked nice was on my wedding day.

I don't cry or get angry, I have to be strong for my family.

What I really feel inside...

I don't feel that I have any identity any more.

Then he comes home to me and I'm this drab, dull, uninteresting woman, surrounded by children.

If I did, you might not be able to see the footprints on my face.

You might think me selfish if I spent money on myself.
I'm a martyr to motherhood.

...sex-proof!

Naturally I'd like to let them know how shallow and self-centred their lives are, but really I long to go out with them and just have a laugh.

Most of my other interests have dwindled away to nothing.

But I also feel like I've taken myself out of the equation and I resent my husband and children for it.

I still want to be a fairy-tale princess.

I just punish them by sulking for days.

How you look

There's nothing more time consuming in life than being a mum. It has a bearing on every waking second. At night, more life is sapped from you when a sobbing child is woken by a wet nappy or a nightmare. In the day, your clothes speak volumes of the silent martyrdom you go through in being the best mum in the world.

Like an air stewardess or a traffic warden, a Mum of Small Children has a uniform. There are so many of you that have fallen into the fleece, jeans and trainers trap, that we are surprised the government doesn't subsidise your look like they do the police force. They should give out haircut ration books for the regularised bob that is just long enough to tie back in a pastel scrunchie, and collectable vouchers that get you your nylon, long-strap, multi-pocket handbag.

What is it that turns you into bland, background beings who have forgotten the sexy woman their husbands once found so attractive? Where is the make-up you used to apply so proudly? What has happened to the legs and cleavage he couldn't wait to get his hands on?

You know they are there, but those tapered jeans, poorly cut corduroys and high-neck, plain T-shirts have erased them from the world.

And these are your smarter clothes! Many of your have resorted to, and adapted in your own way, the Jennifer Lopez tracksuit look, and your colour palette is as insipid and uninspiring as the walls of the delivery room bed cover. Regardless of whether or not they suit you, pastel colours are the only variations in your collection of black, grey and navy fleeces. And you wear these pastels in the obligatory shapeless T-shirt or cropped trouser (the only pant partner to your jeans or cords) or for very special occasions a chiffony, floral print, bias-cut skirt.

In a nutshell, you have faded from your life into a rut of motherhood practicality that has taken away all your individuality. It's time to take back what is rightfully yours – your personality – and re-introduce it to your wardrobe.

Your shapeless cardigan reflects how you are feeling – tired, bland and worn-out.

Wearing no make-up only emphasises the fact that you had no more than four hours' sleep.

Your giant bag is so overstuffed with toys, nappies and emergency, just-in-case items that you can hardly stand up straight. Some people go trekking in the Himalayas with less.

In all this bland beige you'll certainly blend in – with the blenders in the white goods department at Curry's.

Trousers match the non-colour of your top and have a slightly saggy bum as you bought them during pregnancy.

Comfortable shoes need not be drab. You are a mother, not a granny.

How others see you

'She feels everyone else is funnier, wittier, more a part of the group'
– husband

'Friends "eggshell" around her' – Trinny

'She only wears eye mascara if there's a BIG occasion' – sister

'She's not got the guts to change... and I want her to change' – husband

'I would like to see her strut a little bit, to say to the world "I am me"'

– mother-in-law

Dear Friend

When was the last time you got a compliment? Could it have been when you were last pregnant and your friends and family commented on how blooming you looked? Now that you are immersed in a daily grind of school runs, supermarket parking bays and folding buggies it seems a lifetime ago that you actually had a life. Back in those days your predicted future of motherhood was likely to have had the Mills & Boon glow around it: all fluffy white towelling nappies and Labrador puppies playing joyfully with your chubby offspring. Of course you were the softly groomed mother for your kids and friskily clad slut for your man. You could do it all AND get a three-course dinner on the table by eight p.m. Oh, sod it, we have all had those dreams and as any mother will tell you being a 1950s icon of perfection simply can't be done in the impossibly fast world we live in now. But whatever anyone says about you or your clothes, you ARE a Good Mother.

And you wear this label like a badge. You tell anyone who questions your disappearance into bleached-out domesticity that 'my children need me'.

Of that we don't dispute. What we do argue against is the fact that you use your kids to defend your dress sense. It's not their fault that you look as interesting as a bottle of own-label fabric softener. You are not marketing yourself to your best advantage and you have come so far from your original dream that you can't even see yourself any more.

We've established and acknowledged you win 'The Best Mum of the Year' award, but the one person we are concerned about, aside from yourself, is the father of your children. Assuming you are still together, and he hasn't bolted after a brighter member of the female clan, we wonder where the poor guy fits in. We both know what's it's like, and often we are to blame for putting our blokes at the bottom of the food chain. It's hard to fit him in among the piles of laundry, and he says he is understanding of the children coming first.

But be honest with yourself. We have a sneaky feeling that you fear he might be losing interest... 'But of course he'd never leave because I'm such a good mother.'

No? Think again. It's time for you to wake up and smell the freshly brewed coffee you should be making for him. Do you think he's proud of you as his wife? Not as the mother of his children, but as his wife? It could be that he misses the carefree girl he fell in love with and longs for a reminder of her. Of course he loves you, but does he still fancy you? Does he want to rip off your fleece and baggy grey bra? Is he overcome with lust when he sees you in your tracky bottoms? We feel sure you know the answer, although you'll find someone or something else to blame for the lack of sex and attention you get. We do sympathise, but is it surprising that the attraction is temporarily lost when you make no effort with your appearance?

As your best friends have been no doubt hinting to you, it's high time you got your act together. It isn't so hard to think of yourself as well as everybody else. Once you have set your mind to digging out the old you and re-inventing her to suit who you are today, you will find the time to be and feel part of the gang of girlfriends, a tribute to your husband and goddess to your kids. We know you have it in you, you just have to believe it yourself.

Susannah   Trinny
x

The remedy

It's been non-stop every day, we know. Feed the kids, get them dressed, packed, off to school, shop, wash, cook, pay bills. Everybody is so demanding. But what about you? You have a name and an identity much bigger than 'somebody's mother' and 'so-and-so's wife'.

WARDROBE

Wearing clothes that look tired has only added to those feelings of neglect. If you've recently given birth, pack away your lovely pre-pregnancy clothes that don't fit you at the moment. Keep in your wardrobe only the clothes that actually work for you right now. Be grateful to your body for giving birth – don't punish it. Know that you will fit back into your old clothes eventually.

Not everything you own has to be machine washable, but do look for an inexpensive, fitted T-shirt that works for your body shape (Marks & Spencer, Hennes, Gap) and buy several so if one of them gets covered in play paint or fruit salad you can throw it away, guilt-free.

PATTERN AND TEXTURE

Patterns or tweedy weaves are a great choice for stylish coats and jackets. Tweed is particularly hard-wearing. A printed pattern or multi-hued weave will divert the eye's attention from odd stains that you're bound to incur as a mother.

SMART CASUAL

Nobody expects you to turn up at the school gates in a pencil skirt and five-inch stilettos. But a little tailoring need not be uncomfortable. A waisted, three-quarter-length coat still gives you a casual, relaxed look and is every bit as easy to slip over the shoulders as a crusty cardie. Well-cut, flattering jeans can be worn as easily as baggy, shapeless ones. Teamed with a funky belt and T-shirt you will make your children dead proud of their stylish young mum.

COLOUR

Wearing all one colour is usually a bad idea, unless it's beautifully coordinated and exquisitely accessorised. We can't stress often enough the importance of finding the colour palette that doesn't make you look more tired that you already are. Spend a little time experimenting and combining your separates so you won't have to spend hours in front of the mirror each day, trying to figure out what goes with what.

A tailored coat looks casual yet chic and this busy pattern will cover up a few little bits of baby sick or squashed banana.

T-shirts are the most inexpensive yet versatile garment known to woman. Find the T-shirt to flatter your shape, making sure it's a fitted one, and don't be afraid to allow a splash of decoration.

This roomy bag looks great and is just big enough to carry the daily essentials of motherhood without turning you into the Hunchback of Notre Dame.

Accessorising your outfits says 'I do respect myself as an individual'.

These stylish jeans are every bit as practical as your old beige baggies.

Finishing touches

We've seen you. Scurrying out of the door to get the kids to school, no time to put on make-up or jewellery. We're sure we've met mice with more panache. Your children, on the other hand, are dressed in bright woollen overcoats, smart skirts and new trainers. Oh, now we're beginning to understand... your children *are* your accessories.

BAG

We live in an ever-expanding universe. But we are here to tell you that the laws of astrophysics do not apply to handbags. As well as wrecking

your outfit, lugging an overstuffed bag will damage your posture. Try to find ways to downsize everything. A few baby wipes in a ziplock plastic bag rather than the whole brick of tissues. A scrunchy little soft toy will do the job just as well as that life-size baby doll. You can buy juice or water at a shop, as needed. Although back-packs may be better for your posture it's only true if you actually wear them on your back rather than slung over your shoulder. The truth is, they generally look hideous – black, nylon and nasty – and you will only be tempted to fill it to breaking point. Better to choose a good-looking, roomy bag and empty it daily.

SHOES

It's really important to find shoes that are comfortable for the school run, schlepping around the shops and up and down the stairs at home. But you already know that. How about a pair that look good too? These cool Converse trainers say: 'I'm no longer a teenager but I'm still a young woman'. Don't be afraid to stride out in heels occasionally. There are so many wearable heels to be had these days. Try on some cork wedges for comfort or a pair with rubber composite soles.

JEWELLERY

You do find jewellery bothersome, don't you? Even ostentatious? A precious ring would only end up falling down the plughole and the little one pulls on any necklace that you wear.

Try adding a brooch or pinning a lovely silk flower to your coat. Bangles are inexpensive and easy to coordinate with your colours. Even better, your baby will have fun playing with them (almost as good as a rattle) and they're practically unbreakable.

AROMATHERAPY

You've just done a marathon around the aisles at the supermarket and they didn't have half the things on your list. No staff to help you, huge queues and then as you struggled out through the crowds you dropped the eggs. A divinely perfumed aromatherapy roll-on will help you to de-stress. Apply it to your wrists, and then take a couple of minutes just sitting in your car or at the bus stop. Close your eyes and breathe deeply from your abdomen. This small ritual is part of the relaxing process. Repeat this mantra: 'I am the best that I can be right now.'

- For stress and tension, choose lavender and camomile. Lavender is also wonderful for headaches.
- For relaxation, choose frankincense, orange and juniper.
- For spots or minor bumps and scrapes, choose tea-tree and manuka.

MAKE-UP

Do you ever catch yourself in a passing mirror and think: 'Who is that tired dish-rag?' You probably looked great when you got up this morning, but the trials of the day take their toll. Go for the fresh 'no make-up make-up' look. It only takes minutes to cover up the odd spot, and a dab of lip gloss and blusher does wonders to lighten your face. Try to find mini-size cosmetics that you can keep in your bag easily without being weighed down. The products we've chosen here are small and have built-in applicators or can be dabbed on with a finger so you don't need to carry extra brushes around. Refresh your make-up after lunch and mid-afternoon or whenever you feel you are starting to sag. Now catch that girl in the rear-view mirror – gorgeous!

Life tips

Your fairytale isn't over, it's only just beginning. This is the real-life fairytale which you have chosen and you deserve to live it happily. It's only natural that your children are now at the centre of your universe but, equally, you are their sun. Please don't cast yourself in the role of a super Stepford wife. Make sure that you allow time and enjoyment for yourself so that you can be the best you can be, for them. Your children need you, not as a substitute food and money vending machine but as a wonderful individual, who can pass on all the variety of your own experience to guide them into the future.

Find ways to play with your children which also involve exercise for you. Bike rides, power walking with the stroller, skipping and hula-hoop are all fantastic exercise. Doing activities regularly with your kids gives you a better relationship with them and means that you won't have to go to the gym. One less thing to find time for.

You may be feeling exhausted because you have a child who climbs into bed with you every night and wakes you up. Build a little nest bed on the floor of your bedroom and she will soon learn to climb into that instead, happy to know that you are nearby.

Turn resources to your advantage. Baby wet-wipes are the best instant stain removers. And if you spill some juice on the carpet or table, a disposable nappy is the most absorbent thing on the planet.

Don't do for others what they can do for themselves. Your seven-year-old son cannot clean the house and drive to the supermarket but he can make his own bed or prepare a sandwich for himself, and do it with pride, if you show him how.

Go out with your friends and let your hair down, at least once a fortnight. Allow your husband to babysit – he is capable of keeping his own children alive for a few hours, however imperfectly. If you are a single mother, set up a babysitting club with a few other mothers to share the load.

Make time to be alone with your husband as well. We don't mean in adjacent armchairs in front of the telly. Make dates to go out to together, or stay in without the children. Talk to him and listen to him. Romance needs intimacy and shared experiences to survive. If you are really having difficulty finding time, you may have to resort to putting all the clocks in the house forward one hour and telling the children it's bedtime!

When? Having a laugh on a night out with the girls.

Why? This outfit shows that you are a mother of three but still a young woman. Only when the kids are asleep can you risk wearing such delicate fabrics.

TCR 10:47:37:08
PLAY   LOCK

TCR 10:06:41:11
PLAY   LOCK

TCR 10:12:15:05
PLAY   LOCK

TCR 10:15:10:16
PLAY   LOCK

TCR 10:48:50:04
PLAY   LOCK

TCR 10:47:33:18
PLAY   LOCK

Sara found that she loved being the centre o

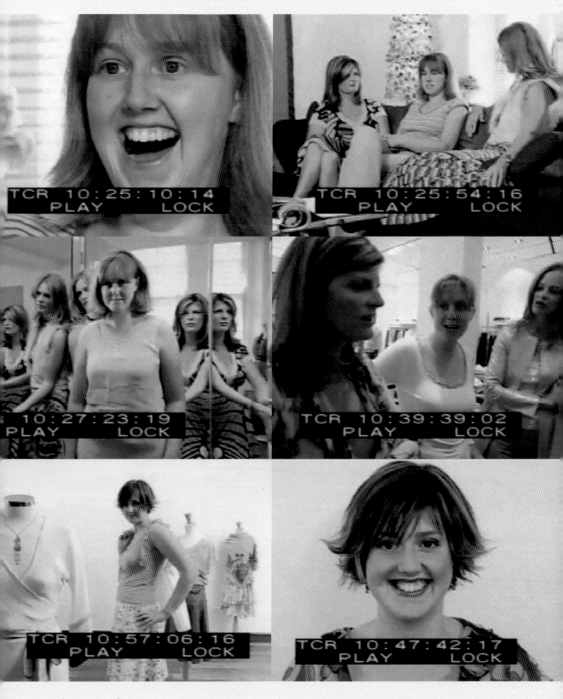

TCR 10:25:10:14 PLAY LOCK

TCR 10:25:54:16 PLAY LOCK

10:27:23:19 PLAY LOCK

TCR 10:39:39:02 PLAY LOCK

TCR 10:57:06:16 PLAY LOCK

TCR 10:47:42:17 PLAY LOCK

ttention. So can you...

Remember

✳ Let your hair down once in a while, both literally and figuratively. Shake out your ponytail and get yourself out to a club with your friends.

✳ It only takes five minutes to put on make-up. Go for a simple, fresh-faced look. Choose products that come with a built-in applicator, or crème-based products which can be applied with a finger.

✳ Go hunting for the fitted T-shirt that is right for your body shape (we talk extensively about body shapes in our books *What Not to Wear – The Rules* and *What you wear can change your life*). Stock up on these, you'll wear them a lot.

✳ Busy patterns or multi-coloured woven fabrics for coats and jackets really help to divert the eye from any minor stains.

✳ Use the resources available to you. Form a baby sitting club. Allow other family members to do their share. They're not perfect either, so trust them and let them make mistakes.

Clothes that are fitted and well cut are every
bit as practical as shapeless, baggy ones. It's just
a question of learning what's right for your
body shape.

 Do activities with your kids that also involve
exercise for yourself. You'll feel great, they will
love you for it and you'll save loads of time by
not having to go to the gym.

 Downsize everything in your handbag. It will
save you money on osteopaths' bills in the
long run.

 You are not perfect and nobody wants you to be.
Allow others to help out and make their own
mistakes along the way.

 Go on dates with your husband or stay in together.
You might have to pull a fast one on your kids - but
that goes to show that you're still smarter than they
are. You two need time alone to keep your romance
alive.

'Look at me

4

boys!'

'AND THEY DO – AS A
ONE-NIGHT STAND'

TRINNY AND SUSANNAH

What I say...

If you've got it, flaunt it!

I always carry a can of deodorant and my make-up.

These pointy nails and heels are very femme fatale.

Most of my friends are blokes.

I just like having a few drinks and a laugh.

I don't need anybody, I can take care of myself.

I get chatted up a lot...

It's important to keep yourself out there.

One-night stands are just a bit of fun.

I dress soberly at work, but when it comes to going out I like
to show off my assets.

What I really feel inside...

Well, I think that's all I have to offer.

At least I'll smell okay when he chucks me out in the morning and a bit of slap will cover up my tears.

Underneath my scary exterior I'm quite defensive, really.

I feel uncomfortable around women.

I'm not sure that I could hold my own in a serious conversation.

I'd love somebody to care for me, but I seem to end up supporting the guys I'm with.

... but I know what they're really after.

There's no good reason to be at home.

Maybe any man is better than nothing.

I feel uncomfortable in social situations, and worry that my personality is not enough.

How you look

It only takes a glimpse of you hanging over the pool table or attempting to keep both almost-exposed bum cheeks on the bar stool to recognise the kind of girl you are portraying yourself as. Your provocative dress looks like you are after one thing and one thing only...

Your tribe has variations in its style of dressing. Some of you dress the tart 24/7. Your clothes during the day will differ little from the swatches of cloth you wear at night. You will probably cover up more, but your kit will still be tight, the heels high, nails long and face brightly painted because you always need to be prepared for that potential pick up.

Then there are those of you whose dressing habits are more vampire like…and not in a vampish way, because vamps are in control of their sexuality. Just like our friend Dracula, your alter ego remains dormant during sunlight hours – instead of a coffin you use hoodies and boyish clothes to bury yourself from male attention. Then, once the sun goes down and the prospect of a drink or two is on the horizon, the strumpet in you emerges.

A night on the town is when you all come together in one happy clan. Then it's tight and short with lots of make-up and all manner of accessories. There's see-through, frosted pink lipstick, peroxide, halter-necks, bare midriffs, belly button rings and very, very tight jeans or trousers. You give no thought to the girth of your thighs, bust size or stomach mass when choosing outfits. So long as the result bares enough flesh or reveals sufficient curves it's okay by you. This look shouts to everyone but yourself that you're up for anything tonight.

Always too tight, this top does nothing to make you look curvaceous, it merely highlights every fold of fat, both on your front *and* your back.

Do you understand the concept of underwear? Its job is to flatter your assets, not ridicule them.

A pussy pelmet skirt looks great in the daytime with flat boots, if you have amazing legs. Worn with impossible heels and less-than-perfect pins you're giving out a totally different message.

Just picking up a variety of garments that are all pink doesn't mean they will work together or necessarily even suit you.

How others see you

'We've got a strippergram in the office' – boss

'If I was kerb-crawling I'd probably ask if she'd take 20 quid' – colleague

'What does she wear? Not a lot' – friend

'She was working with the children, bending over a lot, and a lot of flesh was on show' – colleague

'All she ever does is meet guys who she ends up supporting and looking after' – friend

Dear Friend

Have you ever considered that the way you dress is perhaps doing the reverse of what you think? When you slip into your clothes and slap on the make-up, it is no doubt done meticulously and with a view to the men you might attract. We can see how important looking sexually attractive is to you. If you were invisible to the lads, you would be no-one. And if you left the war paint in the pot you would be sending yourself onto the front line of social acceptance without so much as a bra strap to entice the world. But is dressing like a red light dweller getting you what you truly want in life? Are you happy being the honey pot of the pub? Do you feel loved when a bloke moves on to more permanent lodgings? Is your brazen approach to clothes a true representation of who you are?

Sweetheart, we feel it is such a shame that you dress the way you do. The tight and short of it is that your dress sense is a clear and palpable sign-post of the desperation you have to be loved. Dressing the tart begs the question as to whether you are subconsciously doing it to ward off the kind of man you would like to have a proper relationship with. Actually, we wonder if you use your clothes as an excuse for your single status.

We suspect that deep down you find it easier to blame your trashy style than your insecurity for the one-night stand that goes nowhere. Is the reality that your look harbours a shy girl who's longing for someone to love her but assumes nobody can, because she imagines that all men share the low opinion she has of herself?

While you dress to stand out, to be individual, you would be amazed by the number of women we have come across who, like you, use clothes as a defence. For that is what you are doing. All that effort to attract is in fact a defence mechanism to protect the person who in the past was probably terribly hurt by some bastard. You may feel that person was hurt because she was not worthy, so you now hide her away and show a woman you misguidedly believe men will want. This behaviour may have been going on for so long, that today, being treated like a disposable object is the only kind of 'love' you are aware of.

'Yeah, right, and dressing differently is going to get me the man of my dreams, so that I can live happily ever after in a castle atop the hill.'

It does seem a rather tall fairy story, we know. We also know that in changing your appearance, you will change men's attitudes towards you. It's not rocket science. If you dress like a hooker, one-night stands will always be available. And yes, we know that it feels good to be wanted and indeed makes you feel powerful, but if you dress more the lady a whole new world will open up to you. Finding your man may take longer, because the guy whose eye you catch will be more likely to respect you and want to take things at slower pace, rather than leaping into the sack within five minutes of meeting you. He will be a more genuine type, one that will love your quieter, more unsure side. This is the man you are worthy of. Every girl deserves her knight in shining armour and that includes you. Dress with a little more decorum and that prince will be yours.

Susannah   Trinny

x

The remedy

We know that you're reeling from the shock of even thinking about wearing this outfit so we'd like to explain it to you. You're thinking 'boring', 'conservative', 'frumpy'. We say that this outfit achieves exactly the image you so desire – SEXY.

WARDROBE

There's a lot of preparatory work to be done before you appreciate the benefits of dressing like a seductive, self-assured woman.

Have a really honest look at every single item in your wardrobe. Any garment or accessory that looks like it might possibly be worn by a Playboy bunny is not doing you any favours, those looks are theatrical costumes. When you wear them in the real world they just attract the wrong kind of attention.

UNDERWEAR

We know that underwear is one of your passions, but let it be a private one. Good underwear creates a seductive impression by concealing as much as it reveals.

Go through your underwear drawer with a fine-tooth comb. Throw out anything stained, stretched, or with holes or runs. Next, organise all your underwear, like with like. Even more importantly, from the point of view of the new you, rid yourself of any underwear that was given to you by former lovers, no matter how expensive you think it was.

TOPS

Too-tight tops only magnify and reveal every fold of flesh on your torso. Look at your back view as well as the front – there's probably spill-over there as well. A bared midriff leaves absolutely nothing to the imagination – you have two choices: 100 sit ups a day or cover it up. Find a selection of flattering vests and camisoles to wear under your slinky see-through tops.

SKIRTS

We spend our lives teaching women to draw attention to their best features while distracting the gaze from those which are less flattering. If you have a truly divine pair of pins and a pert butt, then go ahead and show them off in a mini, preferably worn with thick (but not black) tights and flat or low-heeled comfy boots.

DÉCOLLETAGE

A fleeting glimpse of a lacy bra can be gorgeous, but putting all of your goods on display is just another sign that you are dressing 'desperate'. Use a bust cream, and exfoliate regularly to keep the area in mint condition and free of spots.

There's enough on show here to suggest that the best is yet to come.

A row of buttons leading the eye towards your cleavage is tantalising and enormously sexy. This seductive effect can be enhanced even further by dangling a small ornament on a neck chain to point the way.

This jersey dress is figure hugging in all the right places while discreetly glossing over the less welcome bumps.

For women with shapely legs the most chic and flattering skirt length is just skimming the knee. If you have particularly chunky legs stick to longer skirts which will draw attention away from the stumps and up towards your other assets.

Round-toed, high-heeled shoes give a perfect curve to your calf and avoid giving the impression that you might be out to fillet a fish, or a man, with your toe.

Finishing touches

Discretion is your new watchword. Suggestiveness is the new sexy. Toning down your accessories won't turn you into a wallflower. With just a few well-chosen finishing touches you will breeze out into the night feeling like a gorgeous model – and we don't mean the page 3 variety.

TIGHTS

Look at your tights. Are they flattering your legs? If you've been a fan of shiny tights for years you're probably unaware that they're making your legs look like a pair of pork sausages on the run from the supermarket chill cabinet. We swear by bell and book on our fishnet tights. Large nets are great for shapely slim-line legs and the finer mesh are essential to flatter a chunkier limb. For really special occasions seamed tights add a touch of film-star glamour. Make sure your seams are straight and only wear them with skirts to the knee.

If you prefer flesh-coloured tights for daywear, please choose a pair of sheer 7 or 10 deniers that actually enhance the colour of your flesh. In summer, dare to bare your legs. Take a tip from the likes of Nicole Kidman, Renée Zellwegger or Angelina Jolie, all pale-skinned girls who look fabulous, don't you agree? Simply exfoliate and apply a light body oil to those silky shins.

SHOES

Round-toed or peep-toe shoes are so much more approachable than those scary razor points. If you have slim ankles like Susannah, then a shaped heel shows them off to their best advantage. If your ankles are thicker, like Trinny's, go for a straight up and down heel to balance them out. When you do meet your ideal man you will be able to stand toe-to-toe with him without fear of puncturing a main artery in his foot.

BRA

Pay particular attention to your bras. Ditch any that are too small – 80 per cent of British women don't wear the right size bra. The most common crime is to buy a cup size too small and a back size too big. Go and get yourself re-measured. Also get rid of any bras that are stretched or missing a hook. Invest in two different styles of bras. The first, like support pants, is going to give you a fabulous silhouette, it will be lace-free for a smooth finish over your T-shirts, but will probably not be the one you use for seduction. The other category should be a very pretty bra in a tone that you wear a lot so it will work with most of your clothes and look great if briefly spied beneath your outerwear.

SCENT

Perfume goes off after a while and ends up smelling like rancid cat's pee. First, have a thorough clear-out of all those old half-used perfumes from Christmases past and the little sample bottles that came free with a lipstick purchase. If they're still good you can use them to freshen up your car or your linen drawer.

Scent is a very powerful memory trigger. In the morning, after your shower, dab on a little of the perfume you normally wear. Does it make you feel somewhat melancholy, wistful and sad? That may because it is reminding your subconscious of a lost relationship or a time in your past that was unhappy. Those ghosts must be laid to rest.

Your next step is to find a perfume that makes you truly happy. Go around the department store or, better still, a specialist parfumier and try many different scents, not on your wrist but on the little paper tester strips that the sales assistants will have hidden under the counter. Don't be seduced by the packaging, the advertising or the sales girl's patter. Take the strips away with you and keep sniffing them in turn. The perfume's true scent will develop after about half an hour. The right scent for you is the one that instantly lifts your spirits every time you smell it. Finally, go back to the shop and try it on your wrists, again wait half an hour for the perfume to react with your body chemistry before you finally decide to lay your money down. This new scent will become a source of constant delight to you. Wear only a little – perfume is not a substitute deodorant.

HAIR

We're guessing that you go either for bimbo blonde or raven black. Both are very hard on the face and tend to look completely cheap and false if badly applied from a bottle. Professional hair colouring can be expensive and high maintenance, but most good hairdressers offer inexpensive, or even free, model sessions where your hair is worked on by a student – always under the beady eye of an instructor. If you must buy your hair colour from the supermarket shelf, then go for a more muted shade that complements your skin tone. Choose a semi-permanent colour and renew your roots every four to six weeks.

LIP GLOSS

When we look at your old frosted mouth paint we shudder at visions of some poor hapless bloke stuck to your face, struggling like a trapped eel to free himself, then rushing home in a frantic search for his chisel and sandpaper to try to remove the residue. A luscious lip gloss is far more inviting and just plain kissable. Apply two coats with a lip brush and refresh it regularly.

MINI MAKE-UP REMOVERS

Piling new make-up over the old will leave you with a decidedly crusty look. These handbaggable eye make-up remover pads let you wipe away any clinging debris before reapplying.

Life tips

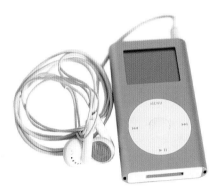

You long for a mate who you can really trust and share all the joy and the hardships of life with. Who wouldn't? But how will you find that special person if you are continually searching in all the wrong places? Loneliness is a state of mind that only keeps you lonely. Look around you and be honest – are you not surrounded by special people? Your family and friends, your children, your work colleagues, your neighbours and the people in the local shops – these are your own community and they really are the most important people in your life. Learn to be your own best person and the right partner for you will appear.

Go out to a club one night in your tracksuit. You probably won't get picked up, but you will just relax and enjoy yourself.

Change your music collection. Delete all those painful songs that glorify suffering and misery. Your crying by the phone days are over. Replace them with some strong, life-affirming tunes and sing along at the top of your voice.

If you think that you might be addicted to the familiarity of painful, unrewarding relationships then SLAA (Sex and Love Addicts Anonymous) may be for you. Pick up the phone, go to one of their meetings and find out more. Don't be afraid, feel proud that you are taking a strong step towards creating your own happiness.

Make a date with your girlfriends. Go to the movies or a restaurant, even camping. Anything that doesn't involve a bar or a nightclub.

Stop running to your singleton friends for relationship advice. You wouldn't ask your plumber for legal advice. The fact that they're single too should be a big hint that this is not their particular field of expertise.

Go cold turkey. Stay in – on your own. Try not to watch TV. Instead, read a book, listen to music, draw a picture or write some poetry. Learn to have fun in the company of one.

If you have a secret list of all the attributes of your ideal partner, please tear it into a thousand

pieces. No man alive can reasonably be
expected to live up to all of the requirements
of your fantasy so you're only setting yourself
up for disappointment. You just don't
know what wonderful potential
soul mates are around the
corner, but you surely will not
recognise them if you're
always looking through the
narrow blinkers of that
impossible list.

When? Lunch with friends,
drinks after work.

Why? This is the way to wear pink
without looking like a bunnygirl.

TCR 10:46:13:03 PLAY LOCK

TCR 10:16:46:07 PLAY LOCK

TCR 10:45:09:17 PLAY LOCK

TCR 10:31:56:22 PLAY LOCK

necklace £98
butler & wilson

dress £125
reiss

TCR 10:50:50:08 PLAY LOCK

TCR 10:46:07:17 PLAY LOCK

Lisa made the journey to sophisticated ar

TCR 10:08:38:22 PLAY LOCK

TCR 10:09:20:01 PLAY LOCK

TCR 10:32:36:14 PLAY LOCK

TCR 10:46:46:12 PLAY LOCK

TCR 10:46:43:04 PLAY LOCK

TCR 10:46:14:01 PLAY LOCK

xy dressing. So can you...

Remember

 Stop searching for your 'other half'. Why settle for half? You deserve a partner who is a whole human being. Be your own best person. Work on liking yourself, enjoying your own company and the life that you have right now. Trust that the right partner for you will appear.

Rid yourself of everything that has unhappy associations for you. Gifts from old lovers, underwear, jewellery, perfumes that conjure up sad ghosts of long ago. They may have cost a bomb, well, that's the price of freedom. They're only taking up space in your head and in your home, bringing you down every time you see them.

 When it comes to bosoms on display, less is definitely more. A tiny flash of pretty bra or a slightly opened button showing just a bit of cleavage hints at what could yet be revealed. This is far more inviting, and exciting, to a man than having a great pair of wobbly melons shoved in his face.

Tear up that list which defines your perfect man. It's only blinding you to the ideal man for your life. If he's human, he will be wonderfully imperfect.

Find a scent that makes your heart sing. In time try to find two different scents, a lighter floral one for daytime and a heavier, spicier perfume for evening.

Enjoy your own company. There's always something to do – gardening, reading books, drawing your cat. Even if you have to build a ship from matchsticks, do something. Waste not one more second of your life moping by the phone.

Cleanse off your make-up (especially mascara) and reapply before you go out in the evening. Lip gloss is far more kissable than long-life lipstick.

Tops that are too tight don't make you look thinner. Instead they magnify every extra fold of flesh on your torso, front *and* back.

Soften your hair. Find a tone that brings your face and eyes alive. It will probably be quite close to your natural colour. If you're not sure then consult a good hairdresser.

Underwear belongs *under* your clothes. It's main job is to support your outerwear and make you look great by concealing as much as it reveals. Don't dress as though you're desperate. Lap dancers are not sexy, merely available.

'I dress old old!'

?But I *am*

TRINNY AND SUSANNAH

What I say...

My clothes are traditional brands, very good quality.

I love dull.

Life does seem very tiring, a lot of the time.

After menopause you disappear into the background more and more.

Bright colours are very wearing on me.

Everything is so loud and confusing these days.

I enjoy pottering around and listening to Radio 4. I can do that and clean the kitchen at the same time.

My back aches.

I don't seem to have time for holidays, so many people depend on me.

What I really feel inside...

I have no idea about style so I stick to what I feel safe with.

I *am* dull.

I've forgotten how to have fun.

I feel that I'm on the hill downwards, that there is no point in doing anything new any more.

I am a faded human being.

I love complaining.

I don't want to interact with real people.

I'm looking forward to a nice lie-down – in my coffin.

They might depend on me but would they want to go on holiday with me?

How you look

Whizz...whooosshh. Wow, what was that?
Oh goodness, it was the world passing you by.
It was life being pulled from underneath you,
because life hasn't got time for those who think
and dress old before they are old.

Don't try and hide behind your premature Bus Pass. We can see your grey bob and shapeless cardies. We can see your faux sheepskin slippers settled by the Lazy Boy Recliner and we've spied those winceyette pyjamas under your pillow.
It doesn't take a magnifying glass either to spot the emerging bristles sprouting from your chin or the un-clipped hedgerows you call eyebrows. Madam (you could never be called miss), you are way old before your grey-ass-time.

Dearest, it is quite crazy that you dress the way you do. It's madness to allow yourself to get away with box-pleated skirts and twin sets. Everything about you is so OLD...so fusty, musty and crinkled. It's all so navy blue and matching. It's all so curtain material, florals, buttoned-up shirts and frilled collars. It's all so clip-on earrings. And those shoes. Those navy, semi, demi court shoes with the sensibly low high heel are tragic. They are a desperate indictment of your cobweb world.

There is no sense of fun about your dress. Not a smidgen of sex appeal. In fact, you ARE the archetypal spinster. You are the virgin aunt who's never had a lay and drinks a tablespoon of cod-liver oil with her cocoa every night. We know it. Your grandma kit tells us everything.

Your condition is just as much about your state of mind as it is about the state of your style. It is either your primness of thought or lack of self-worth that prevents you from looking your best. It's not, as you so often say, because there is nothing for you in the shops. Anyway, how on earth do you know that, seeing as you haven't walked into a decent clothes store since you became addicted to drab?

You are the victim of charity shops and hand-me-downs and as it is mostly other old women who give to charity and do the hand-me-downing, you have turned in to a fogey.

Is your hair colour making your face look careworn and washed out? And the style – it looks like a suburban Farrah Fawcett-Majors.

Your baggy cardie is your safety blanket. One of the most unflattering garments in creation, it gives you a saggy arse and broadens your middle. Keeping your hands in the pockets enhances the dowdiness of your silhouette.

Pleated, high-waisted skirts and dresses. Who did they ever flatter? Even a Greek goddess would look pregnant in this. It's the perennial dinner-lady dress, always in a synthetic fabric and diabolical print.

Is anybody's skin really the colour of these so-called 'flesh-coloured' tights?

Even if you have the ankles of a racehorse they will suffer in these drab flat lace-ups.

How others see you

'She looks 100'
— daughter

'She's sunk into a grey morass of dog-hair-covered yuck' — sister

'She doesn't hold herself erect, she tries to look insignificant' — fiancée

'If she stopped wearing cardigans it would be a *disaster* for the cardigan industry' – brother

'All she needs is a pipe and a rocking chair' – Susannah

Dear Friend

You are probably thinking what a couple of ageist cows we are. How dare we slam the old and infirm! How could we criticise the frail and fragile. Do we have no respect for the wisdom that belongs to the grey generation? Of course we do. But the woman we have described has no age. She isn't a silver-haired widow dressed in black, making lace in the doorway of a small village house in Greece. She could as easily be in her twenties as 78. This isn't about age, it's about attitude.

What happened to sap the life out of you? You don't just go to bed young and wake up with the outlook of someone who has lost their zest. We feel sure that you have had some grief in your life. This could have been the death of a dear friend, divorce, financial troubles or an illness. Whatever the woes, we see that the weight of them has sapped the life out of you, leaving only a husk of your former self, and that these worries are indeed responsible for your drab, drip-dry exterior.

We *know* that you are not NEARLY as boring as you look. In fact, many of you use a sharp wit to flick away any ideas that you might have dried up entirely. But the audience of your comedy routine is a rarefied one, hand picked by you. We have a sneaky suspicion that the likes of your parents and many of your old friends are privy more to your penchant for complaining than your jokes. You need and like having their support for the burdens you carry around. Have you noticed the arrival of statements worthy of Miss Haversham? – 'young people these days'; 'computers are a nightmare'; 'I can't work my mobile phone'. It's not an overt whingeing but more a resigned internal kind of global complaining. Everything is such a disappointment that in your hoary old heart you think it flippant to dress in a fashionable, stylish way when your world is so full of sorrow and loss. You have descended into the depths of partial mourning, but whom are you missing? Could it be the vibrant, exciting woman you kissed goodbye to with the first pair of slip-on shoes you bought?

Becoming old before your time is like living life in a holding bay. You exist, but you don't live. Any form of spontaneity is out of the question, because there is always a dog or sick relative that needs feeding. Holidays! God forbid, you simply have not got the time to go on holiday. What would everyone do without you? The reality is that deep inside, you feel you don't deserve to go on holiday. Well, who the hell told you that? Why don't you deserve to have fun and lead an existence of a free thinker to whom the world can offer everything? Of course you do. You have as much right as the next person to be happy, look wonderful, have great sex and win the lottery. It's time to bring out the feather duster and give yourself a spring clean. With a bit of polish and good hoovering of the cobwebs (inside and out) you can shine. The confidence you gain from positive thinking and a Thumb-up-at-the-World attitude will attract new people like flies and make old friends and family sit up and listen. Swat the ones that try to drag you back down because it is *your* life you are living, not theirs.

Susannah   Trinny
x

The remedy

How old are you? How old do you feel inside? We suspect that you've been feeling older than you really are. This is not a question of years – some women start dressing like crones in their 20s and 30s – it's an impression of being worn-out. We're talking dowdy, not granny-chic. Whether you're 25 or 75, if you dress old and tired, you'll feel old and tired. It's a vicious circle, but we'll help you break it.

HAND-ME-DOWNS

Go through your wardrobe. Where have your clothes come from? Are they really *your* clothes? Or do you find that many of the items actually previously belonged to your mother, your sister, friends or perhaps came from the cupboards of a deceased person, via the charity shop? We are very much in favour of recycling, but you're not obliged to accept other people's cast-offs as an act of self-sacrifice. Those people are probably not the same size, shape or colouring as you so in all honesty their clothes cannot possibly suit you. They're just old and tired. You need to get them out of your life.

HOARDING

There are areas in your wardrobe that are even more prone to stagnation than your clothes. Jewellery, shoes, make-up, tights, hats, nighties and pants (yes, you're definitely a pants wearer, no sexy knickers in your drawers), all of these tend to get hoarded over the years. The point is that there are too many musty old memories lurking around in your wardrobe and not enough fresh air. A really thorough clear-out will produce a great haul for the charity shop, which will make you feel good about yourself, and provide a year's supply of free dusting rags.

REARRANGING YOUR WARDROBE

Take a fresh approach to everything in your wardrobe. Hang your clothes differently, by outfit instead of skirts with skirts and trousers with trousers. Have fun in front of the mirror, creating new looks with items that you never would have worn together before. For example, you may have a pair of trousers that are a little too tight around the middle but still fall beautifully, and a dress that shows off your figure but is not the most flattering length on you. Wear the two together and, hey presto, a new outfit.

An effortlessly stylish cut and some highlights which complement your skin tone will lift greying hair and enhance your eyes.

Stop feeling that you have to cover everything up. Even if you're flat-chested, show a bit more flesh. If your shape has changed over the years or you feel that you've lost your figure, the narrowest part of every woman's torso is under the boobs. Make sure that the dress you choose draws attention to that area.

There's old lady chiffon and there's flirty, floaty, sexy chiffon. You need to feel more feminine and this fabric will help you get there. A pattern that's not floral will jazz you up too.

There is nothing like the shape of the trouser leg to define how old fashioned you are. Wide leg trousers always look more modern. Trousers that fall to the ground also seem to look newer.

Funky beaded flatties bring this look right up to date, yet are still comfortable and affordable.

Finishing touches

Your look has become exceedingly lacklustre. If you allow this trend to continue your only accessory will be a cobweb. It's time to put the sparkle back into your wardrobe – and you.

SHOES

Footwear dates very quickly as heel and toe shapes change from year to year. We cannot, however, recall any year in living memory when beige rubber-soled slip-ons or navy lace-up orthopaedic shoes were the hot ticket. There are some timeless classics like Birkenstocks, Marilyn Monroe stilettos, low-heeled riding boots, Mary Janes and fab Capri sandals. Build a core collection of quality shoes that suit you and maintain them with regular polishing and repairs. Always store them with shoe trees to keep their shape. Supplement these from season to season with inexpensive fashion footwear from the high street.

JEWELLERY

You might have some amazing pieces in your jewellery box. What can make you look old is how you wear them. Get some tips by looking at a few of the latest fashion magazines. Mix classical with contemporary, a pearl necklace with some inexpensive glass beads, for instance. The way brooches are worn today is not the same way that Mrs Thatcher wore them (on the lapel). Re-jigging the way you wear jewellery will really update your look.

SKIN

Underneath all those woolly layers your dead skin has been piling up like dust on your body. Now that you're done with the buttoned-up, covered-up look you'll be showing more flesh and you will want it to be in tip-top shape. Use an exfoliator all over your body, paying particular attention to chest, elbows, knees and feet. Mix four tablespoons of white sugar with four tablespoons of glycerine, add a teaspoon of aloe vera gel and a few drops of orange and lavender oils. Scrub this all over and leave on for a few minutes to work before showering off. Brushing your skin with a soft bristle brush before bathing and alternating hot and cold water in the shower will get your circulation going. Apply a light body moisturiser. At night use a richer cream on your hands, elbows, knees and feet. Drinking eight glasses of water a day will flush out toxins, helping to keep your skin plump and glowing.

BLUSHER

That pale, washed-out visage you see in the mirror adds greatly to your overall feeling of tiredness. It's time to wake up. Exfoliate your face every morning, then sloosh with plenty of cold water. Moisturise and use a light foundation or tinted moisturiser. You're not one for wearing lots of make-up, but you definitely need to bring some colour back to your cheeks. Use a cream-based blusher, on the apples of your cheeks only (just smile inanely to see where they are). Blend it in lightly with the tips of your fingers.

BROWS

Shape your eyebrows by simply removing any stray hairs from under the arch and any hairs growing across the bridge of your nose. Use a good sharp pair of tweezers. Don't be scared to trim them with scissors if they're long and wild or growing upwards.

HATS

You haul out your good hat for the annual summer wedding season, brush off the cobwebs, plonk it on your head and off you go. Stop. Look in the mirror. Does that hat suit your face? Even if you have wonderful bone structure, dark circles or eye bags can begin to take over. Wide-brimmed hats emphasise this. Far better to go for a hat that frames your face or even reduce the hat altogether to a gorgeous floral or feather corsage worn on the head. Don't only wear hats for best.

HAIR CUT

Get with it! You've probably been going to the same hairdresser for years. It's time to try somebody new. We're not implying that your trusted hairdresser is incompetent, it's just that you've fallen into a rut together and you need a fresh objective eye to be cast over those dreary locks. Someone who won't be afraid to take a risk with you and not just give you that same old style that you feel safe with. Do your research by asking any of your friends who always seem to have gorgeous hairstyles. Personal recommendations are always the most reliable. Talk to your new hairdresser about a cut that looks effortless and not overly fussy. Don't be afraid to take along photographs of hairstyles that you like.

GOING GREY

If you're going grey, and it comes to us all sooner or later, do so with good grace. Don't try to rush back in time by reaching for the henna, peroxide or Grecian 2000. It's simply a matter of understanding how to go forward. In fact, our hair does not go grey at all, it loses its pigment and turns white. The grey effect is an optical illusion caused by seeing your original colour mixed with the white.

The trick is to add highlights or lowlights that make the most of the colour you have become. Some will flatter and lift your eyes and skin; others will make you appear haggard. Is your hair an elegant silver ash or just fag ash? If you were naturally blonde then you are fortunate because the white hairs blend in well and can be enhanced by adding a few golden or beige-blonde streaks. If your hair was black or dark brown it is best to add some lighter browns and cool chestnuts to give a chic glazed brown look.

Remember that as you get older your skin also gets paler so do not attempt to add really dark blacks and browns. These hard colours will only make you look drained and bring out any circles under your eyes. Redheads with a warm skin tone should add streaks of rich soft copper along with some warm golden tones.

Life tips

Feelings of decrepitude run more than skin-deep. For quite some time you have been convincing yourself that life is all downhill from now on. Along with that comes a kind of inertia. It's not that you are lazy, just averse to trying anything new. You have sunk too deeply into the armchair.

Shake a leg. Throw off your tweed blanket, arise from the sofa and shimmy on down to your local dance class. Enlist in a class that allows you to dress up, show off and feel sexy. Ceroc! Salsa! Tango! You'll have a ton of fun, meet new friends and feel amazing. Most importantly, you will turn the spotlight on yourself.

You may be carrying around a sackful of worry and grief. This is a heavy burden to bear day in and day out. Maximise the efficiency of your suffering by getting it all off your chest in one session. Write a list of all your troubles, then set aside say, ten minutes at 6.30 p.m. every Friday night and really give it your all. Wail, moan, berate yourself loudly, punch pillows and throw things at the wall – while tearing that list into smithereens. Once that's over, go out to a movie.

If you feel you need a boost, there's nothing better than drinking a raw juice every day. Always use organic fruit and veg if you can get them. Carrot, apple and ginger juice provides age-fighting antioxidants, helps break down toxins in the intestine and is an excellent tonic for the entire digestive system: juice 6–8 carrots with 2 apples (Cox's or Braeburns are delicious) and a one-inch chunk of ginger. The following combination is believed to provide excellent qualities for regenerating and healing tissues within the body: 4 carrots, 1 small handful of flat-leaf parsley, 10 fresh clean spinach leaves (with stalks), 2 sticks of celery. The good news is that it only takes a couple of minutes to make a juice and all the parts of your juice extractor (except the motor) can go in the dishwasher.

Laughter is a fabulous antidote to depression and feelings of helplessness. It is empowering and has actually been shown to boost the immune system. Rent a stack of comedy videos and settle in for a night of laughing until you wet yourself. Stock up on humorous books so that you can go to sleep each night with a smile on your face. A good belly laugh eases muscle tension, empties out all the stale air from your lungs and releases endorphins, your body's natural painkillers. What a tonic.

Do something to get yourself noticed every day, in a positive way. You don't have to go to extremes by bunjee jumping from the Humber bridge. It could be that you voice your opinion in a group situation, wear something bright and colourful to the supermarket, or flirt with the man at the flower stall. Each night write down in your journal what you did to stand out from the crowd and how that felt.

We truly believe you are as young as you feel. Get in touch with your body – hatha yoga and pilates classes are wonderful relaxing ways to gently ease out all those bodily creaks and groans. You will notice a difference after the very first session. As you become more supple you'll hold your head higher and your back straighter. Your digestion will improve, which helps to dispel that sluggish feeling.

Take heed of all the generous gestures you receive in a day, from people offering to help you in small ways to compliments or gifts. At the same time, notice how many ways you find to decline that help or bat away those compliments. Spend the next week learning to accept every act of kindness that comes your way by simply saying the following words: 'thank you'.

When? Winter daytime, for work or shopping.

Why? This outfit includes all your old favourites – leather, tweed, boots and a scarf. It's the way you wear them that creates a youthful, modern look.

TCR 10:48:10:24 PLAY LOCK

TCR 10:31:41:06 PLAY LOCK

TCR 10:33:55:20 PLAY LOCK

TCR 10:33:07:17 PLAY LOCK

TCR 10:43:02:22 PLAY LOCK

TCR 10:52:42:18 PLAY LOCK

Helle stepped forth from the shadows wit

TCR 10:13:28:21
PLAY   LOCK

TCR 10:34:50:02
PLAY   LOCK

TCR 10:48:45:06
PLAY   LOCK

TCR 10:50:02:15
PLAY   LOCK

TCR 10:51:33:05
PLAY   LOCK

TCR 10:48:12:13
PLAY   LOCK

Remember

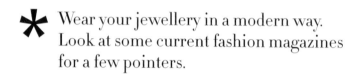 Learn to laugh with others and at yourself.
Laughter is your body's natural anti-depressant.
*There ain't a lot of fun in medicine but there's a
heck of a lot of medicine in fun'* – Josh Billings

**Wear your jewellery in a modern way.
Look at some current fashion magazines
for a few pointers.**

Reclaim your body. Get your circulation and
digestion working with yoga or pilates and
rejuvenating fresh juices. Get into the habit
of drinking plenty of water.

Bring the life back to your skin with regular
exfoliating. If you're on a thrift drive, try the
following: de-seed and peel a ripe papaya, then
purée the flesh with a banana and a dash of
apple juice to make a delicious digestion-
boosting smoothie. Rub the inside of the
papaya skin over your face and body a few
minutes before showering. Papaya is an
excellent natural exfoliator.

＊ Learn to ask for help and to accept it when offered.
Just say 'thank you'.

＊ Go grey gracefully. Learn how to go forwards,
not back, by adding highlights and lowlights in
shades that will revitalise your skin and eyes.

＊ Get rid of the hand-me-downs. Pass them on to
someone they will actually suit.

＊ Update your shoes. Prune them down to a core
of classic shapes, then supplement seasonally
with fun but inexpensive footwear from the high
street stores. All your granny shoes must go!

＊ Have fun creating new looks. Put on some loud music
and hold a fashion parade in front of your mirror.

＊ Dance and sing. If you can't find a dance class, try
karaoke instead. This is your chance to shine in
front of others. Take a risk and enjoy the spotlight.

'I *hate* wear and dresses

6

ing skirts

'YOU DON'T HAVE TO BE THE
UGLY DUCKLING ALL YOUR LIFE'

TRINNY AND SUSANNAH

What I say...

I've always been a tomboy.

I don't have space for a full-length mirror in my house.

As a child I hated wearing skirts and dresses.

My comfort zone is baggy jeans and a big, baggy shirt.

My anxiety levels go up when I even think about going shopping.

Surely you can't go wrong with a pair of black trousers?

I would love to find a man who accepts me just for who I am.

I'd break my ankle in heels.

Make-up, yuck! I wouldn't want all that gunk on my face.

What I really feel inside...

I wouldn't class myself as an attractive woman.

I'm ashamed of my body and I don't want to look at myself.

Puberty terrified me and I wish I was still thirteen.

You certainly won't be able to see my tits and bum in those.

I feel like a misfit in the womenswear department.

All other trousers make me feel huge.

I'd be apprehensive on a date. I wouldn't know what to do, to be honest.

I don't have the confidence to wear them.

Oh, my God, *make-up*! It's completely scary and I wouldn't begin to know where to start.

How you look

From behind you ARE a man. You stand like one in a police line-up. Shoulders hunched, hands behind your back. Your legs are set apart, as though moulded by a lifetime of military service. Your hair is short (even sheared round the neck) or tied back, resolutely out of the way. You get a friendly slap on the back...nothing moves. Not a whisker. You are one solid mass of nylon and denim.

Swivel you round and the frontal image is not much more ladylike. There isn't a scrap of make-up or a fragment of anything to establish you as female. Your boobs swing unhindered in a worn-out bra that is free of support and grey from endless mixed-colour washes, and your hips are hidden by limp tops that erase any sign of a feminine curve.

Looking at you now, it's impossible to imagine that you could ever swap your jeans and polo shirts for, dare we say...no, we don't, not yet. Your modest cupboard won't possess one, because it's stuffed to the gills with repeat football stripes, countless numbers of straight leg jeans, baggy T-shirts and zip-up hoodies. THAT is IT. This is all you have in the clothing department. It's all you wear. You don't require anything else because your wardrobe restricts your social life to football matches and the pub.

The word accessory is foreign to you, but were you to understand it, it would be applied to your baseball caps and trainers. You might well have a handbag, or shall we say manbag, but this will be as sexless as a pick-up line from Gordon Brown. If you work in an office environment your suit – we put good money on it – will be black or navy and as shapeless as cigarette smoke. Peeking into your cosmetic drawer, we will find nothing more than B.O. stuff, an ancient bottle of scent from your auntie, athlete's foot cream and foot deodoriser for those stinking flippers that fester from doing 'life' in trainer hell. Hiding somewhere, there could be a lipstick given to you by a sister or friend in desperation.

Have you ever been to a hairdresser? Or does your brother do it with the kitchen scissors?

This totally shapeless and baggy T-shirt hides your personality as well as your figure.

When you have flawless skin and a great haircut, it's okay to not wear make-up. But if you suffer from a break-out or two it's not fun for people to get too close.

Seen from behind, you could be a bloke.

It's obvious you wear men's jeans. They're too long and too wide.

These trainers look great – on Wayne Rooney.

How others see you

'She buys clothes that won't show the dirt and the grease' – friend

'Chop her head off and that could be Eric Bristow' – Susannah

'Every day she wears jeans. They seem to be sewed onto her body' – boss

'I couldn't tell you what colour her legs are' – colleague

'A pair of jeans, trainers and a football shirt...all the time' – male friend

'It would be **so** great to introduce her to a fabric other than nylon' – Trinny

'I've never seen her attract anybody' – sister

'I'd like to see her comfortable, just looking like a girl' – friend

Dear Friend

Harsh words, huh? If you recognise yourself as this woman for the first time, you are probably feeling pretty awful right now. You will be hurt to think that this is how others perceive you. You will perhaps question it, but deep down you know it has to be true, because looking at Susannah in her masculine garb you see yourself. You know you look butch because people have told you so. You were wounded at the time, but brushed it aside as the twitterings of those with only hot air between their earrings.

The thing is everyone, all your friends, colleagues and family, have been dropping the 'get girly' hint for years. But it has fallen on deaf ears. Part of you looks down on women who make the most of themselves. Actually, you have it in you to see them as flighty flibbertigibbets with nothing better to do all day than spend money on clothes and waste time with 'the muck' they put on their faces.

You protect yourself with the belief that men find them attractive because they are intellectually unchallenging; rather like a weekly soap opera; a sort of lazy entertainment option. Yes, this is a little harsh, but look back to the word PROTECT. This reaction is fear based – a deeply ingrained belief that you don't deserve to be pretty or have men flirt with you.

You pretend you don't want to be like your glamorous girlfriends because you fear you could never be like them. The only way you know to communicate with men is to become a bloke. You are much more comfortable to be one of the boys; hiding your sexuality because you are convinced that not one of them could ever possibly find you remotely attractive. So if they aren't going to fancy you, then you make sure they like you. Which they do – enormously. You are on their team; unthreatening, uncomplicated and totally un-sexy.

Happily for us, but perhaps unhappily for you, you have more than one side to your personality. Hiding underneath your gruff exterior is a small girl who would actually *like* to get her posterior into a tight pair of boot-cut jeans. She also rather fancies the idea of being more like her girlfriends. She would never in a decade of Sundays admit it to a soul, but she is there, waiting in the sidelines of low self-worth. The problem is how to extract her. She is terrified of rejection. She couldn't bear to take the plunge with a plunging neckline and stroke of eyeshadow, then to be ridiculed, turned down and rejected. She feels safe in the knowledge that her masculine stance is the reason men don't go for her. What would it be like to continue being ignored as a woman, even with the whole five yards of glamour. She could never recover from that. The small girl would retreat even further into a world filled only with the Final Score. Drinking sessions would be dropped, because she couldn't face the lads after turning up in what was really a drag costume.

We have a sneaky feeling that you have occasionally donned a pretty top or a pair of heels for a VERY special occasion (like your best friend's wedding), and then spent the entire time squirming with self-consciousness, imagining that everyone was looking at you. Well let them look – and hold your head up high. You will learn to deal with the appreciative glances you receive and ultimately you will positively enjoy the attention. Revealing your femininity is not the same thing as saying 'come and get it'.

The remedy

You really need to take a long, hard look and ask yourself why you have been keeping such masculine clothing in your wardrobe. Could it be you are terrified of attracting attention? Well, don't be. You *are* a woman and should be proud of it.

WARDROBE

Remove and bag up all your ill-fitting jeans, man-sized T-shirts, shapeless sweatshirts, big boots, all bar one pair of trainers, and those hideous white three-pairs-for-a-fiver sweatsocks. Look at what's left and organise it into outfits for different parts of your life – work, evening, smart casual, lounging around at home and the gym. Can you create at least two distinct looks for each occasion? If not, what do you need to fill the gaps?

WHICH SHAPES WORK FOR YOU

However butch you might feel, every woman we have ever dressed has a definable figure. You might feel like you hate your entire body, but there is an alternative way to dress. You can still hide those bits you are very uncomfortable about, but begin to learn to appreciate your good points, and reveal the parts that make you a woman. If you have boobs, long and shapely legs or a pert bottom, don't hide them.

HOW TO SHOP

Once you have discovered what shapes suit you and written a list of garments you are lacking,

take a deep breath and – go shopping. Remember that sales assistants are paid to help you, however intimidating they might seem. Make it a day out and allow breaks for tea and lunch, otherwise it will all get too exhausting. Avoid department stores – there are too many clothes and it can be very confusing. Go to a high street where there are plenty of shops like Oasis, Zara, French Connection, Monsoon. Take all the time you need and only pick out those clothes that you have identified as working for your body shape. To find out which colours to chose, look at *What you wear can change your life*. If you make a mistake, don't panic, take it back. Most stores have a straightforward returns policy.

FABRIC

Be open-minded about fabrics. Avoid your old friends like knitted stretch nylon – and denim. You're probably not yet ready for chiffon and lace. Opt instead for rayon, silk, velvet and wool gabardine. A fine-knit cotton with a little bit of lycra will drape beautifully over your figure and soften your silhouette, far prettier that the heavy cotton knit of your old rugby shirt.

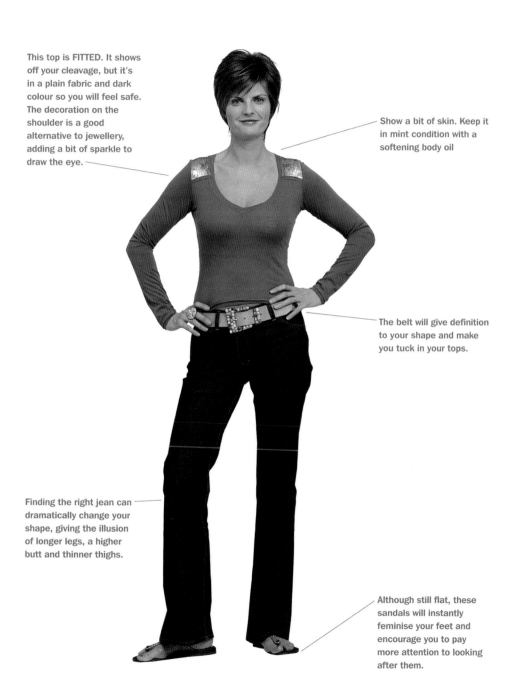

This top is FITTED. It shows off your cleavage, but it's in a plain fabric and dark colour so you will feel safe. The decoration on the shoulder is a good alternative to jewellery, adding a bit of sparkle to draw the eye.

Show a bit of skin. Keep it in mint condition with a softening body oil

The belt will give definition to your shape and make you tuck in your tops.

Finding the right jean can dramatically change your shape, giving the illusion of longer legs, a higher butt and thinner thighs.

Although still flat, these sandals will instantly feminise your feet and encourage you to pay more attention to looking after them.

Finishing touches

It is the little touches that define you as a woman. Not just tits and ass but shoulders, neck, hands and feet. Take a few tips to learn how to show them off to their best advantage.

BELT

In the old days, your grandad wore a belt to prevent his baggy trousers from falling down. Men's belts are designed to be worn by men and will do your figure no favours. For modern women, the purpose of a belt is to define and flatter their body shape. A wide belt worn on the hips disguises myriad stomach folds. If you're flat up top you can wear big chunky buckles, but if you're of the bustier persuasion opt for a more delicate buckle. Unless you're stick thin with a stomach like a draining board, belts worn round the middle tend to cut you in half, emphasising the tummy and enlarging the arse.

RING

You communicate as much with your hands as your mouth and you want us to be favourably impressed by what you have to say about yourself, don't you? However big or small your hands are, there is a ring for every shape. Generally large-boned hands with long fingers, like Trinny's, suit a large statement ring (*never* a sovereign). Smaller, shorter hands, like Susannah's, are better shown off by smaller, delicately worked rings. Wearing the right ring will enhance this most eloquent part of your body.

SANDALS

There's nothing wrong with trainers. It's the fact that you wear them 24/7 that we take issue with. Trainers for work, trainers to go clubbing, trainers to the theatre. Will you be wearing white trainers at your wedding? These dainty sandals glamourise any pair of trousers; wearing them will also force you to get a pedicure and begin to take care of yourself more in areas that will bring out your feminine side.

EYELASH PERM

This is a great beauty remedy for lazy, unvain women like yourself. Take the time every two months to go and have your eyelashes professionally permed at a beauty salon. You will be delighted as your eyes take on a new, more opened up and expressive look.

CONTACT LENSES

Do you wear glasses to see or to protect yourself from being seen? On occasion wearing tinted contact lenses will give you an amazing allure and nobody will be able to tell quite what you've done. They're really worth the trouble.

PEDICURE

Dilapidated feet are just repellent. A little love and care will turn those hideous hooves into enchantingly feminine tootsies. A professional pedicure is a wonderful way of pampering yourself. You'll come away feeling like you're walking on air. Maintain your feet between pedicures with a good exfoliating scrub and a rich foot lotion applied at night (you can wear loose cotton socks in bed, if you're sleeping alone). Keep the toenails trimmed.

Neutrogena

body oil
natural sesame seed

for soft and
supple skin

para una piel
suave y tersa

aceite natural
para el cuerpo
a la semilla de sésamo

250 ml ℮

BODY OIL

Another great time saver, this lovely light oil can be rubbed into your body as you get out the bath and your skin is still damp. It takes half the time of applying body lotion and is instantly absorbed. It also smells delicious so you won't have to resort to fragrance.

MAKE-UP LESSON

None of us was born knowing how to put on make-up. It is an acquired skill. If you've never learned, then you really need to be taught how to wear make-up. Avoid the department store cosmetic counters where the state of the sales reps would put anyone off ever wearing it – unless planning a night out at the local transvestite bar. Instead, book an appointment at a specialist make-up store that offers education in great application techniques and a nude-look face. Try Bobbi Brown, The Body Shop or Mac. Take advantage of their make-up lessons, but don't feel pressured into buying excessive amounts of slap. Only buy what you feel you will really use; the basics should definitely include mascara, concealer, blusher and lip gloss. Ask lots of questions about how to choose colours that suit your skin tone. Don't be afraid to get the consultant to show you how to do it for yourself. Using quality brushes for eyes and lips makes all the difference to applying make-up with speed and precision. Remember – you can always buy the brushes separately.

MASCARA

Even if you wear no other make-up at all, you have got to wear mascara. Why? Because that's what all GIRLS do.

Life tips

For too long you've been feeling uncomfortable in the world of women, yet you're not a man, really. It's time for you to step out with confidence and pride in who you are. Walk tall!

Put on your new confidence-building outfit. Then go into places that would normally intimidate you – a super-smart shop in Bond Street, for example. You don't have to buy anything. In fact, you are under no obligation whatsoever. It's just a shop. You're just browsing, thank you. If you do need help you will ask the sales assistant. Resist your urge to bolt for the door and keep looking until you're satisfied that you've seen everything you came in to see. The point is that you have the right to go wherever you please and not feel uncomfortable or pressured.

You're really going to have to grit your teeth to do this. Stand naked in front of the mirror and take a good look at your body. What do you hate? Why? Now notice all the things about your body that you do like. Look at your arms, your skin, your hair, your teeth, your eyes, your ankles, your backside. Actually, you have quite a lot of assets, don't you? Stand up straight and look yourself in the eye – doesn't that make a difference to how you regard yourself? As you begin to find yourself more attractive, chances are so will everybody else.

Wearing your new feminine look, go away for the weekend somewhere where nobody knows you and try it out. See how people respond. Notice if your persona is different. Chat to new people and be who you would like to be. You're never going to see those people again so you can be whoever you want for this weekend.

Okay, you can't bear to spend hard-earned cash on all those yucky, girly cosmetics. Try making your own! Honey has been known as a beauty aid since Cleopatra's day (and she was no tomboy). This toning mask will help to smooth and moisturise your skin. In a food processor blend 1 peeled, cored apple with 1 tablespoon of honey until smooth. Pat the resulting goo onto your face and allow it to work for 15 minutes while you soak in the bath. Rinse off with warm water and a flannel. For a great cleansing scrub: combine 1 tablespoon of honey with 1 tablespoon of finely ground almonds, 2 tablespoons of dry oatmeal and enough lemon juice to moisten the mash. Massage this gently onto face (not your eyes), neck and chest in circular motions, then rinse off with warm water. Wear a shower cap to avoid getting sticky clumps in your hair.

Learn the art of body language. Are you aware that if you stand in a room full of people with your arms folded *nobody* will approach you? Instead, adopt an open posture with your head up and your arms by your sides. If you're particularly interested in someone, try to catch and hold their gaze for about three seconds (any longer will feel uncomfortable, for you and for them). Do this about three times and the other person will by then be open to being approached, or may even approach you first.

Invite some girls to lunch. One will be a good friend (she will support you). The others will be girls who you have always felt slightly intimidated by (they will scare the life out of you). Tell them about how you have felt about them in the past and ask them in turn about their fears. You will be very surprised to find that they have vulnerable sides too.

When? That scary lunch with girls who you've felt intimidated by in the past.

Why? You'll look great and feel totally self-assured in this ensemble. It's feminine but not in the least bit silly.

TCR 10:48:00:10
PLAY   LOCK

TCR 10:03:54:17
PLAY   LOCK

TCR 10:27:23:15
PLAY   LOCK

TCR 10:40:05:08
PLAY   LOCK

TCR 10:55:42:04
PLAY   LOCK

TCR 10:56:30:15
PLAY   LOCK

Lyn emerged as a confident, beautiful butt

10:08:11:18
PLAY   LOCK

TCR 10:14:06:06
PLAY   LOCK

TCR 10:48:31:09
PLAY   LOCK

TCR 10:40:28:03
PLAY   LOCK

TCR 10:48:50:12
PLAY   LOCK

TCR 10:48:01:06
PLAY   LOCK

. So can you...

Remember

 Take a good long objective look at your body, naked. We all have bits we *don't* like. Focus on the positive, which parts of you do you find most attractive? Figure out how to show off all your best attributes. In time, you will even fancy yourself.

 Have a lesson in make-up application. Book an appointment at a specialist make-up store. They will always offer you products, and goodness knows you need some, but you are not obliged to buy anything.

 Flirt. Outrageously! Try it out at first in a place where nobody knows you, then take the plunge and flirt with someone at one of your regular hang-outs.

 Keep your body glowing by exfoliating regularly. Use a very light body oil on your chest, arms and legs if they're going to be exposed.

 Don't be afraid to go shopping. The sales assistants are there to help you. Who cares what they might be thinking? You are a customer and have the right to be there.

* Give yourself a luxurious treat with a professional pedicure.

* 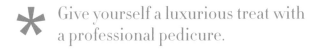 Gen up on the art of body language: it says more about you than an entire autobiography could describe.

* Make your own beauty treatments. It's fun and gloriously messy. Once you've cleaned up the bathroom you will emerge looking and feeling fabulous.

* Reveal your vulnerable side to people who you've felt intimidated by in the past. It may be scary, but you will probably see a whole new, and pleasant, side to them.

* Make it a rule to wear mascara. Every time you leave the house.

'Some peo

I'm colour

some say sl

eccentric...

7

ple say
ful,
ightly

'SOME SAY *COMPLETELY*
OVER THE TOP'

TRINNY AND SUSANNAH

What I say...

I'm scared of Drab.

I love bright patterns and stripy things.

It's really nice to have that bit of fun element. I don't want to lose that.

This is my personality – here I am!

If you wear dull you just blend in.

If you're wearing a bright coat or something different you'll stand out.

My clothes are a reflection of me.

Everything I pick up is pink.

I would never wear black, brown or olive.

What I really feel inside...

I'm scared you'll think *I'm* drab.

I don't want to grow up.

I'm desperate to have people like me so I put on a show.

My zany image is all there is to me.

I need to feel like I'm the centre of attention at all times.

Just like wearing a suit of armour.

But who am I?

Underneath I'm really angry and I don't know how to express it.

I feel they might bring me down and dampen my mood.

How you look

Have you ever considered the fact that as you emblazon the supermarket checkout with your eye-watering colours, fellow aisle trawlers raise their hands to their mouths not to stifle a yawn, but to suppress a snigger. They didn't realise the circus was in town.

We look at you and see a woman (only just) submerged beneath a violent storm of clashing patterns and colours. We see a blob of a body distorted by voluminous garments, misshapen from overuse. We know a human form exists, camouflaged among the exploding patterns. The bottom line is that you look like someone that belongs to a touring troop of pantomime artists. It's not you who we see, it's your clothes. And the clothes are letting you down…badly. The truth is that you don't look like a cheerful bird of paradise, but rather a bad taste blot on the landscape.

You misguidedly assume that the garishness of your dress sense compensates for wearing shapes that don't flatter your body. Weird colour combinations like acid yellow and vivid azure blue degraded by a washed-out peach remind us of a ball of mixed colours of play dough that has been rolled in the hands of a four-year-old. Big zebra prints teamed with leggings and black and white kitchen-tile earrings do NOTHING to make you more appealing. Over-sized shirts, jackets, coats and sweaters act as an alarm, alerting us to your dissatisfaction with parts of your body. The combination of big clothes and chaotic patterns and colours does little to enhance your standing in the world.

We know you are used to your death-defying dress sense, but it really doesn't make you a more interesting person. The truth is that people who don't know you are laughing at you behind your back. Those who do know you, and care about you, feel exasperated. They want to see a shift in style, have dropped hints, but you don't listen because at the end of the day it's down to you. You won't change until you see yourself for what you have become.

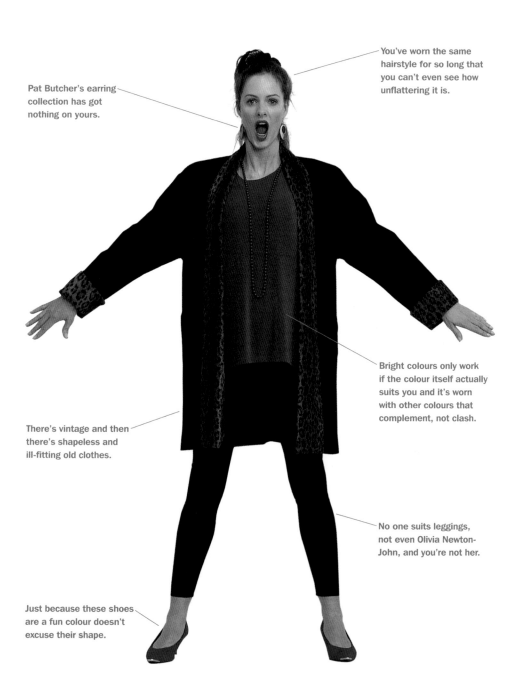

You've worn the same hairstyle for so long that you can't even see how unflattering it is.

Pat Butcher's earring collection has got nothing on yours.

Bright colours only work if the colour itself actually suits you and it's worn with other colours that complement, not clash.

There's vintage and then there's shapeless and ill-fitting old clothes.

No one suits leggings, not even Olivia Newton-John, and you're not her.

Just because these shoes are a fun colour doesn't excuse their shape.

How others see you

'She's completely individual, completely off her head...she's just mad' – boss

'Find the most hideous two pieces of clothing and she'll put them together' – friend

'She's been in the dressing-up box again' – Susannah

'When she comes into the office every day we just look at her and go "Oh, my God – what have you got on?"'– colleague

'I don't know why she likes childish things like the rainbow coat and the Shaun the Sheep bag, but I do know they definitely need to go' – best friend

'We're embarrassed to have her work on reception' – colleague

'When working with children, dressing like Noddy is probably quite helpful' – boss

Dear Friend

So you think by dressing up as a psychotic budgerigar that the world is going to be fooled into thinking you are a bubbly, assured, fun-loving girl with not a care in the world. You believe that by looking like a 1980s children's TV presenter everyone will see you as alternative, a little eccentric. The ostentatious colour coding and ship-in-full-sail shirts will make you as approachable as a cartoon character. Everyone loves you because you are so much FUN. Of this, we have no doubt. It takes guts and a huge sense of humour to put on what you wear each day. The thing is we know that you are not always laughing. You're not gleeful as you put together another catastrophic outfit. You may feel at home in your costume, but that's because your dress sense has become your personality.

What is it that you are feeling inside? Are you really this over-confident person with more front than Selfridges or are you, as we suspect, someone a little vulnerable and shy, who would rather hide behind a caricature. You see, we can tell how you feel about yourself by the way you dress. We know from our experience with fellow flamboyant dressers that you are aware people look at you for the wrong reasons. You detest drab colours so you continue with your addiction to psychedelic hues. But is your trip really giving the right message?

Let us tell you about one of your wacky-dressing sisters who came to us for help. Her boss thought she was a strippergram on their first meeting and the HR department refused to put her on reception because her appearance didn't match the corporate image. Her husband, adorable and mad about her, knew how insecure she was about her appearance. He knew the real story; that she felt too ashamed to go to the pub with him. She knew she looked clown-like but was so certain her personality could not stand alone as a glittering asset that she had to enhance it by dressing up.

Shyness is a common trait here and it may be that you, too, are covering your bashfulness with costume bravado, and you could be scaring off some really great people with this wall you put up. Your loud-mouth exterior might benefit from a break, while the more timid you gets a chance to breath. People are far more drawn to others who are true to themselves. By exposing your vulnerability they will love you all the more.

Most of us are as scared as you when it comes to revealing ourselves because we are all terrified of rejection. You frighten people away before they even make it to first base. They have no idea of the sweet, slightly fragile you that lurks behind your smokescreen. By toning things down, you will tune in to a new type of person who will be interested in you, rather than the fancy-dress outfit.

We feel your current state of dress is misrepresenting you, but we don't want to turn you into Jane Eyre. Your love of colour is something to be celebrated. We simply suggest you retune your appearance so that you have the courage to tell the world who you really are. We want you to feel attractive and proud to be you.

Susannah   Trinny
x

The remedy

To be truly, successfully, eccentric you cannot wear clothes that are too of-the-moment. Your way of dressing is not about fashion – you create your own style – but it is about educating your eye and standing out as a stylish individual rather than an escaped extra from the Christmas panto.

WARDROBE

Get EVERYTHING out of your wardrobe, everything, and lay it all out on the floor. We always suggest that you enlist the support of a friend for this difficult process.

Never yet worn: this might be quite a large pile and it will contain some fabulous pieces of clothing, but there are reasons why you're not wearing them. If the colour doesn't suit you or the shape doesn't flatter, it has to go. The rest can stay only if by the end of this session you have got a clear idea of how to make them work.

Too young: you're like a magpie when it comes to anything that is extrovert, bright and fun, but these items are usually in the younger sections of the stores. Individual pieces might add a great accent to an outfit, but check that you are not too long on ponchos, skinny scarves, batwing tops.

Too small: if it's too small for you NOW, get rid of it. This is about stripping your wardrobe back to a core of garments that *all* look fabulous on you.

Synthetic: synthetic fabrics do not age well and, to be frank, they can start to smell. Only keep synthetic items that are in mint condition.

Top 5 items: think of what people have most complimented you on. Is it an outfit or is it a specific item? Take that jacket, top, skirt, dress or trousers and figure out why that item works for you. Try to replicate that across the board. This is a useful way for you to discover what really flatters your shape and colouring.

COLOUR

The art to clever eccentric dressing is not to sink into dreary black and beige, but to find colours that clash well together. For instance, hot pink and bright yellow go together like ice cream and sardines, but hot pink and orange bring out the best in one another. To help you master this art, look at *What you wear can change your life*.

PATTERN AND TEXTURE

Just as important as colour for the successful eccentric, but you have to know which part of your body to wear it on. Wear the smallest patterns and sheerest textures where your body is largest. Cover the smallest parts of your body with the largest print and the chunkiest textures.

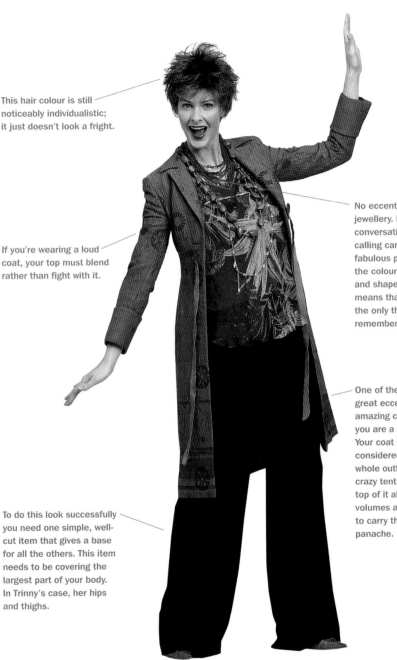

This hair colour is still noticeably individualistic; it just doesn't look a fright.

If you're wearing a loud coat, your top must blend rather than fight with it.

No eccentric wears petite jewellery. It is your conversation piece, your calling card. Making your fabulous pieces work with the colour of your clothes and shape of your body means that it won't be the only thing that people remember about you.

One of the keys to a great eccentric look is an amazing coat, especially if you are a larger eccentric. Your coat should be a considered part of your whole outfit, not just a crazy tent thrown over the top of it all. It speaks volumes about your ability to carry things off with panache.

To do this look successfully you need one simple, well-cut item that gives a base for all the others. This item needs to be covering the largest part of your body. In Trinny's case, her hips and thighs.

Finishing touches

When it comes to accessories, you really must pace yourself. Your clothes are festive enough already without adding an entire Christmas tree on top. This isn't just some dull, restrictive rule dreamed up by Trinny and Susannah. Too many bits of glitter and baubles direct the gaze all over the place so that instead of attracting the positive attention you so crave, people end up looking the other way only to hide their bewilderment.

COATS

No army ever marched under a banner as inspiring as your coat. In a way, it is your flag and your armour. We see your coat cutting a swathe down the high street long before you arrive and unless you bother to take it off at some point, we may never actually see *you* at all. When a garment is as loud and attention seeking as this it's critical that you get it right. You may absolutely adore your purple velvet robe with the peacock on the back, but does it actually work with your suit? And whatever size you are, your coat still needs to be fitted under the bust.

When you get dressed, put on your coat, pick up your handbag, then check the whole ensemble in front of the mirror before blowing out of the door.

JEWELLERY

This is something to encourage gasps of admiration rather than incomprehension. If you wear lots of big, bold necklaces there's no need for earrings as well. Remember to wear jewellery that flatters the shape of your neck, chest, arm or hand. If you have an long, elegant neck, then you can get away with a pair of chandeliers dangling from your ears, but long earrings will only emphasise the stumpiness of a shorter neck.

A big-boned forearm can support a chunky cuff, whereas a slim, dainty wrist is better enhanced by a selection of more delicate bracelets or bangles. The only purpose of jewellery is to draw the eye of the beholder to a part of your body that you want to show off.

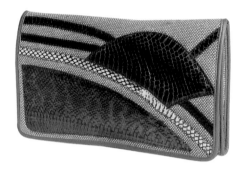

HAIR

We bet your hair is not drab and we love you
for that. You live to colour your tresses – orange,
blonde, black, red or even a multitude of hues
all at once. Our observation is that if you choose
to have an eye-catching bonce, you must
maintain it well. There is nothing more tacky
than a crowning glory of flaming locks with an
inch of black root growing through. Of course
not even a Maharani could keep up such high-
maintenance hair every day. It is for those
bad-hair days that wigs were invented.

VINTAGE HANDBAGS

Luckily for you, a lot of ladies in the last century
bought handbags, then used them only once or
twice before putting them away in the attic for
posterity. These dear-departed dames were your
handbag fairy godmothers. Nowadays, women
put their daughters' names down at birth on the
waiting list for the latest designer purse, which
will be considered beyond the pale only one
season later. A vintage handbag will show that
you're definitely not one of the herd. If you visit
a specialist dealer it is still possible to find a
vintage handbag of superb quality and a fraction
of the price that the same workmanship would
cost today.

EYE SHADOW

Coloured eye shadow can look gorgeous if skillfully applied. Once again it's a question of co-ordination. Choose hues that complement your outfit and blend, blend, blend! With your dazzling hair and outfit you can get away with coloured mascara as well. Between lipstick and eye shadow it's an either/or situation. If you want to draw attention to your eyes, pile on the eye make-up, but at the same time simplify the lips with a nude-look lipstick or gloss.

LIPSTICK AND BLUSHER

Putting on brightly coloured lipstick and blusher does not necessarily make your face look bright and young. In fact, if you're not careful you will achieve exactly the opposite effect. Very strong-coloured lipsticks and blushers can totally drain the life out of you if they're wrong for your skin tone. Go for a professional make-up consultation to figure out which colours enhance your skin and eyes.

SHOES

Trinny positively covets any form of footwear that sports a sequin, beading, gold trim or is even festooned with flowers, but NEVER with trousers that clash. If your shoes are stunning, keep the legwear simple.

Life tips

You've been hiding behind those dazzling, zany outfits for so long that we've been blinded to who you really are. It's time to give your inner self a chance to shine.

You are a woman with a passion for colour

and pattern, but you have not developed a sense of how to create harmony out of what captivates and fires your imagination. Attending painting or design classes will really help you to develop your eye for colour and beauty. Start today by getting yourself a small bound book of plain paper. Each day draw, paint, collect or photograph one image that catches your eye. Don't worry about how good your technique is, your image for today could be a leaf you've found in the street or a picture torn from a magazine. Just do it. You will be creating a wonderful visual journal of your life.

The weight of clutter around you is doing more than taking up space in your house, it is weighing heavily on your peace of mind. Everywhere you look there is unfinished business. That half-knitted sweater, old photographs you were going to sort out. Piles of...stuff! Among all the assorted bric-a-brac and papers yet to be filed, you have squirreled away many real treasures such as drawings by your children or that precious teacup which belonged to your grandmother. But how can you enjoy them when they are just mouldering in corners, gathering cobwebs and dust?

You need to organise the mother of all spring-cleans. Separate the things you truly love, the things you truly need and all the things that you are holding on to through feelings of guilt or fear. If you can't find good homes for the latter category, bin them. Put the things you need where you can easily find them, and display the things you love where they can be properly admired and shown off to others.

It is likely that the way you've been dressing is a reflection of the way you feel inside, in a word – chaotic. Make time to meditate. This will seem impossible at first. But if you make it your priority you will be able to find a ten-minute window each day. This is not something to do after you've taken care of everybody else and done all the chores, if there's time. This is the key to you keeping your individual soul alive while at the same time being able to deal with all those demands placed on you. It is not selfish. You cannot possibly give to others if you are running on empty yourself.

Take a day out with yourself and people-watch. Just sitting and letting the world go by is wonderfully inspiring. See what can you tell about passers-by that you've learned from this book. From the window of the coffee shop on a busy street, who do you see? Armies of black-clad worker ants? What can you tell about the woman at the next table, and that couple in the corner? Go to places where you can unobtrusively (if that's possible for you) hang around. Try an art gallery. Is it a different crowd you see? Fascinating, isn't it?

When? Work, or coffee with friends on a 'bad-hair' day.

Why? You can get away with wearing a wig, so why not?

The new Michalina felt much more profe

nal and powerful at work. So can you...

Remember

 Choose colours that clash well together. Rich turquoise sits fabulously with a bright lime green, but mixing it with black just kills it dead. A painting or design class will help to develop your eye.

 Check yourself in a full-length mirror *wearing your coat and carrying your handbag* before you leave the house. Your coat is an integral part of your whole outfit.

 Wear the smallest patterns and sheerest fabrics on the largest parts of your body. The big prints and chunkier fabrics will look great where you are slimmest.

 It's time for the big clear-out. You probably haven't done it for at least a decade and it will be difficult, even painful. Get one or two friends to help. Hire the village hall if you must. Sell, donate or give away everything that you don't absolutely love or need. Once that's done, display your real treasures in your home with pride.

 Learn which pieces of jewellery flatter and draw attention to the best parts of your body. Save the decorations for the Christmas tree. For more great tips on how to wear jewellery have a look at our book *What you wear can change your life*.

* Coloured hair requires constant maintenance. If it's a special occasion and you're having a bad-hair day, try wearing a great wig or hairpiece.

* Take time to meditate. It's a great way to clear the head and release your creative spirit. Sitting in a park or art gallery and watching the world go by can be a form of meditation.

* It is still possible to buy beautiful, good-quality vintage handbags for a fraction of the price of this season's designer equivalents. The very best ones get snapped up straight away – by handbag designers! Find a knowledgeable vintage handbag dealer and make her your best friend.

* Bright lipstick and blusher will totally drain the life out of your face if the colours are wrong for your skin and eyes. Book a session with a professional make-up artist to discover which hues best complement your colouring.

* Real style is the ability to reflect all the positive aspects of who you truly are inside through how you dress and present yourself.

'Well, I *have* been for years'

married

'OH, *THAT'S* WHY YOU
LOOK LIKE PART OF
THE FURNITURE'

TRINNY AND SUSANNAH

What I say...

I'm so busy all the time.

After so many years of marriage what do you expect?

My husband doesn't want me spending money on clothes.

Beige brings me out a bit.

If I have to go anywhere special, I rummage around and pull out one of my old favourites.

I feel that I should dress my age.

I don't want to feel I'm an embarrassment to my children.

Fashion seemed so much simpler in my day.

Suddenly, my husband seems old. But I don't feel old.

It seems like all the excitement has gone from my life.

What I really feel inside...

If I'm always busy I don't have to think about my own life.

I have moments of feeling utterly disappointed, but I'll never admit it.

My husband controls my life and I allow him to. It's easier that way.

I'm not a colourful person.

I'm apprehensive about buying new clothes. I seem to buy the same thing over and again.

But I don't know what age to dress.

They're absolutely merciless if I don't conform to their expectations.

I want to feel 'with it', but I don't know how.

There are so many things I still want to experience.

We don't have sex anymore.

How you look

We've been searching for a while now, but you are nowhere to be found. It seems you have blended into the background of domestic inertia. Your skirts match the curtains and the dishcloths get mixed up with your shirts. You play it ultra safe in terms of your appearance.

If we were to peer into your wardrobe there would certainly be a plethora of clothes inspired by an image you have of your mother. Not the carefree, slinky-hipped hippie of the '70s, but the woman she became once you were a teenager. Your clothes are the very same ones that you despair of or despised because they made your mum look ordinary. Well, hello… take a look at yourself. You don't exactly shine forth as a beacon of fabulousness. Far from it. Indeed you are decidedly mumsy.

More than anything, it seems you have lost any sense of being anything other than a conduit for other people's welfare. This has resulted in the disappearance of your sexuality. You dress to work on your family. It's sensible kit for you all the way. Yes, you do look loveable, approachable and warm. You are completely unthreatening to anyone, even the family dog. This is great for the mum who has been married a lifetime and is resigned to slipping into middleagedom without trace.

But what about YOU? What about the woman who still has flashes of sexual longing rather than hot flushes of retreating hormones. Don't you feel depressed when you get asked for a fresh glass of wine at a party because you are dressed like the waitress in a non-toxic black skirt and harmless white shirt? Don't you want to scream when your husband doesn't even feel your presence in a room, let alone notice you are actually standing next to him?

Well, the blame is not all his because he has seen you in that floral sack for the last ten years. It's time to update your wardrobe and inject some fine pheromones into shelves that have held lacklustre clothing for far too long.

Your hair never looks like you just emerged from the bedroom – more like the broom-cupboard. It is neat but SO boring.

Is this top:
A. Flattering?
B. Interesting?
C. Sexy?
D. Practical?
E. None of the above!

Why bother with a handbag when you could just as well carry a hessian sack?

A pleated or elastic-waisted skirt will make even Cinderella look like a pumpkin, while the mid-calf skirt length worn with court shoes gives a stumpy look to thicker legs and makes slim legs appear spindly.

Chunky-heeled black shoes give any outfit an air of being old-fashioned and past-it.

How others see you

'She needs to realise that she's actually got something going for her. She might not be a young flower but she's still beautiful' – boss

'I'm not coming out with you if you're dressed like that' – husband

'The last time I saw her looking sexy? I can't really put a date on it' – friend

'I'd love to see what she could look like if she just put a little more effort in' – son

'Never, ever looks nice' – colleague

'She probably has the impression that I don't fancy her because I don't compliment her on her clothing and hair, but she couldn't be further from the truth' – husband

Dear Friend

You have been married for – how many years? Your child-bearing days are now behind you as you hurtle full speed towards what is traditionally considered mid-life. Is this a crisis for you? Probably not, as you are so used to being considered part of the furniture by your family. Mid-life crisis doesn't enter your world because you haven't put yourself first for decades. It wouldn't cross your mind to think you could still be attractive to other men, but you do long to be noticed by your complaisant husband, who loves you in the manner of his favourite chair. You were once the centre of a vibrant household, but as that household fragments your role becomes diminished. You have given yourself willingly and wonderfully to your family, but in the process life has rather lost its spark. The pyjama case is empty, the fridge of life bare.

It's so obvious that you feel like you are taken for granted, but don't blame others because it is you who has allowed yourself to be picked off like a left-over carcass. Your family have forced you into the mumsy look, but it is you who has accepted it without complaint. Your unappealing dress code has rendered you unexceptional. The needs of others stick to the static of your mixed-fibre clothes. As you no longer feel independent and womanly, it's nice to be needed. You can excuse a lot about yourself and the rut you are in, because your family needs you.

There is, however, a great divide between need and want, and being wanted is where we have to get you. To be needed is okay, but so do we need a cleaner, a cook, a chauffeur, part-time PA, answering service, trainee nurse. These are all roles that you seamlessly assume when required. The last person you are thinking about is you because the whole damn household, goldfish to boot, all come before your good self.

Most of you identifying yourselves with this chapter will be in your 40s and 50s. You have a comfortable marriage, children who have or are soon to flee the nest and a nice home. Life is dependable and predictable. There are no surprises to knock you off guard, no zigzags to your flat-line life. WE WANT TO SHAKE YOU OUT of this torpor. You, my lady, are at a crossroads. You can choose to continue on your path of skimming the surface into social and sexual oblivion or you could turn to mutton and dress like a lamb. Staging your disappearance and running off with another man might take your fancy, but is that really what you want? The option we recommend is re-discovering and re-establishing your sex appeal so that you have the other men panting, but you choose to discard them for your refreshed marriage and status as Goddess in the eyes of your own husband and children. THIS is what we call being wanted. It's being desired and admired, emanating sparkle that everyone, even your bolshy teenagers, will want to reflect in.

The remedy

For years now you have been dressing to please everyone else, believing that your glory days were over. Your husband might have been reassured because you were completely unthreatening to his ageing process. But it's up to you to keep you both young and get some va-va-vroom back into your relationship and your life.

DRESSING SEXY

Like everyone else, you must re-evaluate your wardrobe. Take every item that you consider to be sexy. Now, how small is that pile? Are there items you would like to wear that you feel your husband does not approve of? Why do you let him control you like that? Just because you are a desirable woman doesn't mean you are going to run off with the plumber – not necessarily!

Dressing sexy is a question of confidence, of feeling proud to show off your best assets.

Generally, a woman's butt holds up better than her tits. If you have a great bum, choose skirts and trousers that hug it gently. Another great turn-on is a fabulous pair of shoes that flatter the ankle and the calf. It is amazing how many men (and women) are secret shoe fetishists.

JEANS

Are your jeans high waisted, slightly tapered and bought from Marks & Spencer, or an old pair of (not 501s) Levi's? Get rid of them. Turn to the notebook at the back for our jeans shape advice.

YOUR QUALITY JACKETS

Over the years you have collected a large number of quality items: jackets by Windsmoor, Jaeger or Caractère, an Armani suit, your Aquascutum coat. These are the items that age you the most. The worst culprit of them all is the short-sleeved jacket. The fit is roomy, the shape boxy and the overall impression is the sartorial equivalent of Radio 2 – middle of the road. All these must go.

You need to change where you shop. Stay away from the second floor of ladies' fashions in the department store. It is the kiss of death. Instead, hit the high street and look in stores like Jigsaw and Monsoon – they understand how to dress a woman in clothes that are not just fashion for fashion's sake but are cut to suit your shape.

Try on a jacket a size smaller than you normally buy. You'll discover that you suddenly look thinner, taller, and have a waist! Who cares that it doesn't do up or you can't fully extend your arms. As long as you can get your wine glass to your lips, you're set.

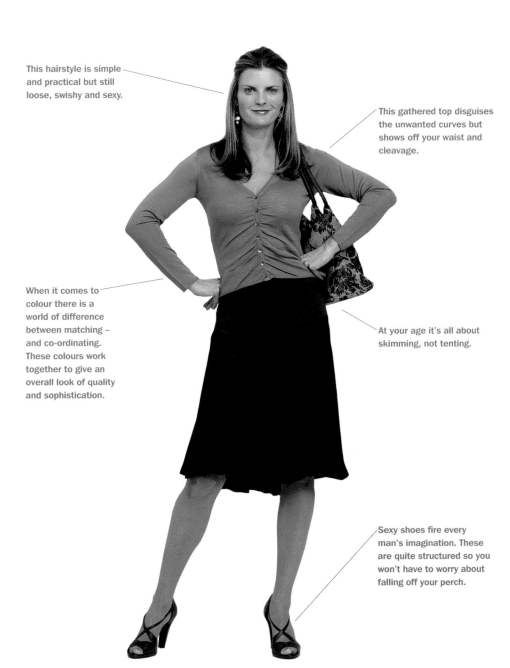

This hairstyle is simple and practical but still loose, swishy and sexy.

This gathered top disguises the unwanted curves but shows off your waist and cleavage.

When it comes to colour there is a world of difference between matching – and co-ordinating. These colours work together to give an overall look of quality and sophistication.

At your age it's all about skimming, not tenting.

Sexy shoes fire every man's imagination. These are quite structured so you won't have to worry about falling off your perch.

Finishing touches

We're sure that you've replaced your worn-out cooker and re-upholstered your sofa when it got tired and dilapidated. Yet you have persisted with a make-do-and-mend attitude to your own appearance. It's high time to give yourself a fresh lick of paint.

HANDBAG

Your handbag is an accessory, as well as a convenience. It should complement your outfit. Possibly the number one fashion crime committed by women all over this land is buying one black handbag and one beige shopping bag and wearing them with *everything*. Look for handbags containing colours that will work with a lot of your outfits. Better to have a selection of inexpensive bags from Oasis, Accessorize and Marks & Spencer than just one expensive, but black, handbag.

LIPS

As the years creep up on us so do the creepy lip lines. It's a big mistake to wear bright lippy which will seep into the cracks, leaving you with a decidedly Frankensteinian look. Take a cosmetic stain and apply it with a lip brush. Then use a lip plumper like Pout Plump or DuWop Lip Venom. The colour will stay on for hours. If your pout begins to shrivel, reapply the lip plumper a few times throughout the day.

UNDERWEAR

You no longer have the body of a twenty-year-old but you're still all woman. It is so important for you to *feel* sexy – and nothing feels sexier than silk and lace next to the skin. You may feel that gorgeous bras are not comfortable, but that is probably because you've been wearing the wrong size for years. Get yourself properly measured, then invest in some inviting undergarments that will make you feel girly again.

LEGS

Find the skirt length that flatters the shape of your legs. If your calves are thick and your ankles chunky, you can look wonderful in a full-length skirt. Don't just save these for evening wear. Team a long skirt with a T-shirt and flat flip-flops for a dreamy summer's day look. In winter, cover your legs with comfortable knee-length boots and wear them with a three-quarter-length skirt. If your calves are shapely and your ankles slim, the most flattering skirt just skims your knee. Forget about the mid-thigh skirts you wore in your twenties. Even a thoroughbred racehorse gets slightly saggy knees once she's over thirty-five.

SHOES

You seem to buy the majority of your shoes in the sales. You still opt for quality and even buy multiples of the same style, but it's so old-fashioned. Dated shoes can so easily make you look past it and frumpy. If you suffer from heavy calves you are doing yourself no favours. If you have great legs, your choice of shoes is even more tragic. There are two new types of footwear that are going to take years off you, Puma's Mostro trainers (the ones with the velcro criss-cross strap) and low-heeled, elasticated leather boots from Hobbs. The former you can wear with your new relaxed sweat pants and low-cut jeans, the latter with the three-quarter-length skirt you used to wear with your heavy court shoes.

HAIR

There is only one thing you have wanted your hair to be – out of the way. Practicality ruled and 90 per cent of the time your tresses were tucked behind your ears or restrained in a big clip. Your trips to the hairdresser have been for maintenance only. Shear off a few split-ends, a quick blow dry and then it's back into the deadly grip of the elastic band. Try tying back just the top section to create a style that is swishy, yet still keeps your hair out of your face. In the evening, a ponytail just will not do. Shake it out, baby. If your hair is feeling a bit flat, it's nothing that ten minutes with the curling tongs won't fix. When it comes to hair, loose women are sexier.

EARRINGS

With your pearl studs and your teeny tiny gold neck chain the effect has been decidedly Princess Anne. Now, she is an admirable horsewoman but hardly a pin-up girl. Again, earrings are a really inexpensive way to update your look, if you are prepared to entertain the idea of ditching the diamond and pearl studs and trying some inexpensive, but more decorative earrings. Choose something that picks out some of the colours in your outfit.

Life tips

In the past you were a bride, a wife and a mother. Treasure all the women you have been, but keep moving forward. There's a big difference between resigning yourself to stagnation and accepting who you are now.

It's time to shake yourself up by doing the totally unexpected. What daydream have you always harboured that would just knock people's socks off? A parachute jump perhaps? Sailing across the Atlantic? Voluntary work in Sudan? Do something today to find out how that would be possible. What is the first step? Pick up the phone or get on the internet. Many charities have schemes whereby you can raise much-needed funds while realising your dream. You won't do it tomorrow, but your achievement will be one day closer. As your scheme starts to shape up, be prepared to encounter strong opposition, especially from your children. They're used to your role as their comfortable footstool. You can bet that all your friends will be cheering you on from the sidelines though.

Sex shops are no longer sleazy. In fact, they're no longer even called sex shops. Visit one of these modern erotic emporiums or fantasy boudoirs and you will realise that sex is not just for students and newlyweds. Everybody is doing it! You don't need to be seen slinking around Soho in a dirty mac, these shops are now in the high streets. And even if you're not yet ready to stride brazenly through the door, you can visit them on the internet. Coco de Mer and Agent Provocateur have websites selling stylish sex toys and gorgeous underwear. Ann Summers will organise a party in your home.

We are bombarded day in and day out in magazines and advertisements with images of perfect womanhood. Many women report that, although their husbands can't keep their hands off them, they themselves no longer feel sexual because their bodies don't measure up to the impossible ideal. They do not believe that a woman with a big bum or soft tummy could possibly be considered attractive. Not so! Sexual attractiveness is not defined by pert tits and butts. It's a confidence job. Instead of beating yourself up with images of the unattainable you need to reinvent your sexual fantasies. In fantasy you are the object of all desire and totally in control of every detail of the situation. Take some time and use your imagination. Where the mind leads the body will follow. If you believe yourself to be sexy and gorgeous, your inner confidence will soon rub off on him, so to speak.

Get into the frame of mind of putting yourself first. Make a commitment to putting aside 10 per cent of your household budget each week for your make-over fund. This money must be used to buy yourself a whole new look. It might mean a week's enforced vegetarianism for your family, or no ice cream for a month. Well, it's good for them – and it's about time they sacrificed something for you. Build up your fund for three months, then go out and blow it all in one day.

When? On a much-needed hot date with your husband.

Why? This outfit will take years off your marriage.

TCR 10:10:46:03
PLAY   LOCK

TCR 10:10:24:09
PLAY   LOCK

TCR 10:41:18:13
PLAY   LOCK

TCR 10:35:21:04
PLAY   LOCK

TCR 10:46:58:13
PLAY   LOCK

TCR 10:51:10:08
PLAY   LOCK

Lynda gained a new level of self-confidenc

TCR 10:17:08:14 PLAY LOCK

TCR 10:33:41:15 PLAY LOCK

TCR 10:35:26:19 PLAY LOCK

TCR 10:46:02:08 PLAY LOCK

TCR 10:52:36:12 PLAY LOCK

TCR 10:46:35:02 PLAY LOCK

nd respect from her family. So can you...

Remember

 Just because your clothes have quality labels, doesn't mean they look good on you and it's no excuse for hanging on to them. Go shopping in some high street stores.

* Fabulous shoes drive men crazy.

* You don't have to play tennis in your new jacket. Its most important attribute is that it's cut to give you a waist. Emphasising the waist makes us all look younger.

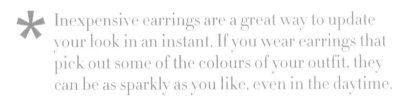 Inexpensive earrings are a great way to update your look in an instant. If you wear earrings that pick out some of the colours of your outfit, they can be as sparkly as you like, even in the daytime.

* Everybody is having sex these days, even married women. Check out one of the modern, stylish sex shops. See if you can get your husband to come with you too.

Do something unexpected and knock everybody's socks off. Don't worry if your children disapprove, your friends will be full of admiration.

 Take your jeans out of the garden and into the restaurant by teaming them with a super-smart top and casual heels. Find the right jeans to flatter your shape and wear them with pride.

 Have confidence that your body is desirable. You are still all woman. Fresh sexual fantasies are key to building positive feelings about your attractiveness. Sexy underwear really helps as well.

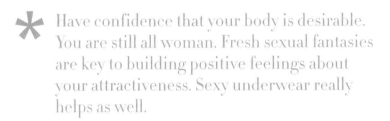 Applying a combination of lip stain and a lip plumper will give you a natural looking, long lasting pout.

 Loosen up your hairstyle. Swishy hair is very sexy. Try spending ten minutes with your curling tongs.

'You're not what
you wear h

9

ody unless

abels'

'BUT DO YOU REALLY
WANT TO BE A WALKING
BILLBOARD?'

TRINNY AND SUSANNAH

What I say...

It's important to *be* somebody.

I'm loud and proud – so don't mess with me.

These sunglasses cost £300.

Check out her cheap trainers.

Oh, I managed to get that latest Prada handbag, didn't you?

I'm dedicated, I've been on the Hermès waiting list for ten months.

Looking at my friend in her Primark copy, I just feel sorry for her.

Putting on two pounds can ruin my day.

It surprises me how many things in my wardrobe have never been worn.

What I really feel inside...

Inside I feel like a nobody.

I suffer from toxic shame.

I'm terrified of my credit card bill.

Making others feel small makes me feel bigger.

I need to always be the first.

I love the thrill of the chase, but once I've succeeded it leaves me feeling empty.

I've got the real thing, and I have to let you know.

If I don't maintain my image my boyfriend might dump me.

I need to buy something every day to fill the hole.

How you look

With all those names strapped to your body you might as well be carrying a sandwich board up and down the high street, advertising the fact that you have money but don't know how to spend it in a classy way.

But looking like you've got cash is part of your dressing remit, isn't it. You want people to know you can afford the power brands. You want your best friend to be slightly jealous that you have the latest Marc Jacobs handbag in limited edition orange. You might have blown a month's wages on it, and failed to honour your direct debit to the mortgage company, but you DO have the handbag. Once the readies have dried up you resort to your fake Louis Vuitton clutch and the Rolex you picked up on a beach in Bali.

Labels are everything to you and just so long as you have at least one, and preferably several, upon your person you feel complete…

When we see you bedecked in expensive clothing labels in an obvious way we recoil.

To us, a woman who wears her brands on her sleeve, her head, her feet, over her eyes, has a sense of greediness as opposed to a sense of style. All those footballers' wives who acquire sudden wealth dress to death in the latest hot items. This is fun when done in moderation, but when the latest bag, sunglasses, trainer, fluffy bootie, hat and coat are worn en masse they become too much. You, too, are hell bent on being seen to beat the Jones's. It's like you have taken the pages of every major designer label's advertising campaign and wallpapered yourself in them from head to toe. Suddenly these items, often individually beautiful, become cheap and tacky.

You've flat ironed your hair for so long that you just can't see the 3 inches of split ends this addiction has spawned.

Trust you to choose a label where the whole garment is a walking advertisement.

Is this T-shirt benefiting you?

Just because the skirt matches your coat doesn't mean it's the right shape for your body.

You may as well just use the carrier bag from the shop, the amount of free advertising you're giving them... but you do that as well!

Even at the tips of your toes you are advertising a designer brand.

How others see you

'She thinks she looks great, but I think it looks tacky' – brother

'She's so worried that if she puts on a pound he'll dump her' – friend

'The designers should pay her... for advertising space' – Trinny

'Shops for Britain' – boyfriend

'She's all bold and loud on the outside but underneath I think she's not all that confident' – mum

Dear Friend

Clothes are like an addiction to you, but it's not just any clothes. No. We are talking über labels: Burberry, Gucci, Prada, Dolce e Gabbana. To you these names are uplifting, exhilarating and seduce you into a false sense of being someone. The thing is, however, we see them way before we see the person wearing them, and by being too overt they act as a branding iron, stamping insecurity all over your body. Brands are your drug of choice, and if they ruin you at least you'll go to your grave with style. But is your method of dressing stylish? Is it imaginative? Does it show flair and individuality? Or is it a neon light of competitiveness and low self-esteem?

What is interesting about you is that the condition of your bank balance doesn't differentiate you. If you are togged head to toe in chic Prada, complete with accessories, or in Adidas sweats, Nike trainers and Burberry baseball cap, you will still have the same underlying desire to elevate yourself above the person you believe you are. The good thing is that you feel you deserve these clothes. The bad thing is you need them even to step out your front door.

Why have you become so dependent on these brands? We would assume that they are filling a void in your life. You are part shopaholic and part label tart. The hit of buying something new is a potent high. It makes you feel powerful and in control.

The truth is, though, that you are not in control at all. You are not spiritually present when you pay for yet another pair of designer jeans. If you were you would halt, consider your ten other pairs and put the eleventh pair back on the shelf. But you don't. They are taken home and added to the denim family. Then the initial thrill of the buy quickly evaporates.

This is when your spirit plummets. You feel deflated, guilty and rather silly to have yet another duplicate jean. The void is still gaping. The purchasing hasn't changed your day. You need to do it all over again.

For you to break free from labels you must look at which part of your life is empty. Try to remember the times when you felt comfortable being yourself and recall what was different. Were you going out more? Was your relationship different? Did you have one? How was work? Did you have a project in your life, something to look forward to? This is a really important exercise to help you understand yourself and find out what you want from life, then realise that clothes just aren't the appropriate substitute. Once the light bulb illuminates what is lacking in your world you can change your shopping methods and douse down the big brands.

Susannah   *Trinny*
x

The remedy

We're not saying that you can never wear lovely designer clothes. Just learn how to wear them in a way that will cause others to admire your look rather than resent you for it.

TURN THE ADVERTS INTO CASH

Go through your wardrobe and take out every item that has a label on the outside or an all-over design that identifies it like a flag. You have probably kept the original bags and boxes so pack them all up nicely. Now ask a geeky friend to show you how to sell them on the internet. There are millions of magpies who collect such trinkets and they're all hanging out on eBay, just waiting for you.

As this probably amounts to half of your wardrobe, you stand to make a substantial few quid. You will probably realise between 5 and 40 per cent of the original cost of the clothes, depending on their age, state of wear and how much of a one-minute-wonder they were to begin with. This might seem little compared to what you shelled out originally, but remember that it is 100 per cent more than they're earning lying unworn in your closet. You get the added benefit of relieving yourself of the guilt caused by staring your shopaholism in the face every time you open the cupboard door. Scatter a few flowers and shed a few tears, then run down to the bank with your cheque.

BENEFITS OF THE HIGH STREET

Stop buying the same thing over and over. You need to discover some new looks that allow you to relax and be yourself. Experimenting is not so scary if the odd mistake sets you back £25 rather than £250. High-street chains will often mimic a designer original but make it more flattering for the average woman's body shape rather than the catwalk supermodel. Zara particularly excels at this. The trick to wearing high-street clothing is to mix it up with your designer pieces so that you look like you haven't made quite so much effort.

HOW TO BUY VINTAGE

The thrill you will get from wearing a timeless one-off original will far exceed anything that bagging the latest fashion piece can give. There are many different ways to buy vintage pieces, according to your budget. Please turn to our notebook for details.

Really look at what you're buying. It might be fabulous but too big. Can it be taken in? If you have a generous chest that flat-fronted 1920s dress might not suit you, but try turning it around the other way so that the deep V is now at the front and it can look stunning.

A vintage fake fur is funky and stylish and will never go out of fashion.

This top is from the high street. By mixing it with the designer jeans and the vintage coat you've created an outfit that says 'I'm an original'.

Anyone can see this is a great bag. It doesn't matter who made it, what matters is who chose it and put the whole look together.

Great jeans do cost money, but they don't have the maker's name written across the backside in rhinestones.

These shoes look amazing but it's the design that speaks volumes rather than the logo.

Finishing touches

You've really gone to town with necklaces, belts, handbags and shoes that are covered in logos. It might be more honest just to wear £50 notes pinned to your lapels or gold bullion bars around your neck. Great accessories add a touch of class when they are beautifully designed to enhance the part of your body on which they are worn.

HAIR STYLING

There is more than one hairstyle in this world, but you don't have to throw away those expensive ceramic straightening irons. Here's how to create fabulous messy, sexy just-got-out-of-bed hair. Pile your hair up on top of your head in a big clip. Work in sections of about one inch, starting from the underneath layer of your hair and working towards the crown. Take a flat section at the roots between the ceramic surfaces of the straightening irons, now twist the irons and at the same time, pull them s-l-o-w-l-y towards the ends of your hair. The smaller the section, the tighter the ringlets, and the slower you pull the irons through, the better curl you will get. Don't try this with non-ceramic irons or you will risk singeing your hair.

SUNGLASSES

What's attractive about these sunglasses is the way they flatter the shape of your face. They don't sport giant gold logos on the sides to distract all attention and blind the beholder. Friends can now kiss you on the cheek without fear of being knocked unconscious.

VINTAGE JEWELLERY

By hunting out quality vintage jewellery you will build a collection of truly one-off pieces that will help you to create an original look. Visit markets and vintage fairs to learn how to get the best deals. Study new role models to inspire you. Women like Nicole Kidman and Angelina Jolie always look stylish without needing to cover themselves with bling.

HANDBAGS

Handbags are the most versatile way to complete your outfit. We know that you love them, but you have been choosing your handbags for their status symbol value rather than for how well they complement what you're wearing. Try to build up a mix of expensive and inexpensive bags so that you have the right one on hand for every occasion.

It's also great to do your bit to support the fashion industry by buying innovative bags from young new designers. Seek them out by visiting small independent boutiques and even market stalls. After all, that's where the big label designers go for new ideas. A unique handbag shows that you have a great eye for fashion rather than a magpie's eye for a fancy label.

SHOES

When it comes to shoes the general idea is to make your legs look long, your ankles slim and your feet sexy. If you get misled by coveting a shoe for its label rather than its shape you will compromise your ability to flatter. Long legs with slim ankles look great in shoes with an ankle strap and a slim heel. If your legs are shorter the ankle strap will cut them off and add to their stumpiness while a slim heel only emphasises thick calves. Better to choose chunky heel or wedge to balance the calf and a low-cut shoe to give the illusion of longer legs. Stop being led by the label alone.

MANICURE

Those long, square-cut, white-tipped talons look cheap and fake – even though they might have cost a bomb. A really good French manicure on short, shapely nails suggests that you have understated class. Worn with one eye-catching ring that suits the shape of your hand, the overall effect is elegant and seductive.

BELTS

Belts are another great way to give an individual finish to your look – or totally ruin it. If you wear an obvious belt, never wear a big necklace. Belts are best worn over something that is on the plain side and needs brightening up. A top that is embellished with beads or sequins does not need a heavily decorated belt as well.

Life tips

I want you to like me!

Sunglasses get lost, handbags sag, necklaces break, clothes go out of fashion, cars rust, houses burn down. The message is: don't love anything that can't love you back. A wise man once said 'Love people, use things'. We think he was a very wise man indeed.

Helping others is a sure-fire way to take care of vague, gnawing feelings of emptiness. Volunteering opportunities abound so start by ringing your favourite charity and asking what you could do. You don't have to become Mother Theresa, but try to choose something hands-on rather than simply writing out a cheque or attending a fund-raising lunch. One afternoon spent rattling a tin, driving an elderly neighbour to the shops, planting a tree or helping out in the local youth club will put a smile on somebody else's face.

Is your wardrobe balanced according to your life? Your outfits have consisted of two extremes, super-smart nightclub wear at one end and tons of designer track-suits and trainers at the other. But does your life consist only of

parties and Pilates? Every Sunday morning check your diary to see how many different looks you'll need for the week, then take time to play around with mixing up things to create new outfits. Bear in mind coordinating colour (for guidance look at *What you wear can change your life)*, mixing high street with designer and vintage clothes, and choosing unique accessories as the crowning glory of your individual look. Once you've decided on your new looks, hang them together as outfits, with the accessories draped around the hanger. Most importantly, when the event arrives, don't have a last-minute panic attack. If the outfit felt right on Sunday it will be right on the night, even if your insecurity tells you to get changed 15 times and go out looking like a billboard at Piccadilly Circus.

Do something fun and very messy. Go paint-balling or enrol in a papier-mâché sculpture course. How about planning a holiday camping with your friends in a muddy field? For laughs it beats a five-star resort hands down.

Learn to want what you have by writing a gratitude list. Sounds unbearably corny, but this process unfailingly opens our eyes to how rich our lives really are. First thing in the morning take five minutes to write down just ten things you are glad to have in your life. Be specific – you might think of 'the beautiful tree outside my window' or 'my pert butt' or 'my son's painting that he made me at school'. Tomorrow write down ten different things. No more, or less. Do this every day for a week. We promise that soon you will be struggling to hold yourself back from listing a hundred things a day and wanting to tell the whole world what an amazing life you have.

Write this message on a piece of paper 'I want you to like me'. Now stick it on your mirror.

If your mania for shopping has left you with credit card debt it can be unbearably stressful. You are tempted to forget your worries for a few hours – by going shopping! It's a vicious cycle, but you can get help to break it. Debtors Anonymous is a self-help organisation which deals with compulsive debting, overspending and under earning. Check out a meeting or an on-line group. It's free.

Practise acts of selfless kindness. Do something to help another person every day but, here's the hard part – you're not allowed to tell anyone what you've done. But you are allowed to write it in your journal to make yourself feel proud.

When? A smart drinks party or event.

Why? This vintage dress is simple yet stunning and you can be sure that nobody else will be wearing it.

The label queen never puts herself forward for Trinny and Susannah's TV show. She thinks she looks amazing covered in logos and trinkets.

The denial is total.

Remember

✳ Count your blessings. List just ten things every morning. You will be delighted by how it changes your perspective on life.

✳ It is so easy to sell stuff on the internet. You won't be wearing all those logos anymore and a nice cheque will soften the pain of parting from them.

✳ Mix high-street garments with stunning designer pieces and a bit of vintage for a truly individual look that is entirely of your own making.

✳ Wearing vintage is a clever way to make your look unique. You can find incredible items that, because they have stood the test of time thus far, will probably never date. Choose pieces that you can wear with pride and the confidence of knowing nobody else will turn up at your birthday party in the same outfit as you.

✳ Get messy. Organise an event with your friends that will leave you covered in mud, paint, dust and grime and just aching with laughter. Nothing to wear? Try a boiler suit.

On Sunday look at your diary for the week and create outfits that are appropriate for every occasion. Then hang them together so that you are ready to get dressed and out the door without a second thought.

 Shift the spotlight off yourself and on to others. Give a little bit of your time and energy to volunteering. Try doing a good turn for someone every day, but don't tell anyone you've done it.

 Buying innovative handbags and jewellery from emerging young designers shows that you have a great eye for fashion and are not afraid to demonstrate the courage of your convictions.

 If you have credit card debt there is help. Get in touch with Debtors Anonymous, a self-help group for those struggling with debt, overspending and under-earning.

 Mess up your hairstyle. Soft, tousled hair looks way more human than the identikit flat-ironed Barbie look.

'I really don't
about cloth

t care
es'

'OR IS IT YOURSELF
THAT YOU DON'T GIVE
A DAMN ABOUT?'
TRINNY AND SUSANNAH

What I say...

I have three jumpers and seven pairs of trousers, four of those are tracksuit pants.

I've got more important things to think about than clothes.

I love these unbleached hemp trousers.

It looked good in the catalogue.

Buy a bra? How are you supposed to choose? There are thousands.

If I put a dress on I don't feel comfy.

I'm not materialistic. This coat could last me the next twenty years.

I don't care what people say about me.

I just chuck everything in the washing machine on the hot cycle.

What I really feel inside...

I don't deserve nice clothes.

You might not take me seriously if I wear fancy clothes.

And my hair shirt.

It will fit right in with all the other tat in my house.

My tits have all gone to pot anyway, so why bother?

Because then I might have to shave my legs.

I have a poverty mentality. I don't believe there will be enough for me.

I would be devastated if they said it to my face.

I just don't care about myself.

How you look

You could be considered a natural beauty if the natural side hadn't been taken to the extreme, having never come close to a bristle brush, let alone a blow dry. We could pass you off as a rather eccentric intellectual. The female negative of Einstein...all dishevelled and wispy hair.

You look like your clothes are borrowed from the local scarecrow and they have the same scaring-off effect on anyone remotely sophisticated or with a whiff of glamour about them.

We could forgive you for your foam-soled, library-creeping shoes in neutral beige. We could also ignore your drawstring trousers that clamp your waist like a bulging vein. A screen could shield us from your 'good warm' chunky sweaters that distort your body like a funfair mirror. Your weather-beaten face, which has never had so much as a swipe of make-up applied to it and has a hearty, ruddy feel, could be called fresh, but reminds us of an earthy, beef stew. But we don't forgive or ignore because we know this 'don't care, won't care' attitude is a façade.

Out of all our women described in this book, your wardrobe will be the smallest. It shines in its lack of ostentation or anything verging on pretty. The only patterns to grace your hangers are checked or a floral print as used by super-stores and market stalls for ready-made curtains.

Your shoes for the most part are canvas or plastic, not for any particular responsibility to cows or other leather-producing animals, but because they are cheaper and, let's face it, you would rather sink in silage than spend money on yourself.

Your underwear is a shrine to your monastic lifestyle. Anyone would be hard pressed to tell your pants apart from wash-cloths and dusters. The elastic has gone on most of your knickers, creating a particularly interesting VPL. They are too loose to cut the butt, but the elastic has turned crispy from too much tumble drying, giving it a crinkled, seaweed effect. This is disastrous under your polyester and lightweight slacks. Your bottom becomes disfigured as though marred by some peculiar scar. Moving the eye up to tit-level, one can see clearly that you have never been fitted for a bra.

In conclusion, you have put yourself bottom of the style chain from the inside out. Hypothetical ditches are fabulous hideouts but not great for living in. Isn't it time to haul yourself out, hoick yourself up, uplift those sagging breasts and point them in a new direction...forwards and a little frivolous. You never know, you might enjoy it.

How can you believe your hair is so unimportant? Lank, greasy hair is a total turn-off.

Spectacles are your only accessory. Have you ever bought a pair that really suit your face?

A white T-shirt is one of the building blocks of any woman's wardrobe, but it should be a *woman's* cut white T-shirt.

There is one word that sums up your style – baggy.

You don't wear big jeans every day, sometimes it's sweatpants. How long is it since your legs have seen daylight?

The only wardrobe-related decision you have made today is whether to wear trainers or heavy boots.

How others see you

'Her hair is completely out of control. I don't know whether it's mown once in a while when her husband does the back lawn'– colleague

'On a scale of one to ten? Minus one' – male friend

'She needs to respect her body enough to dress it better'– Trinny

'It's almost like she hasn't bothered getting dressed' – Susannah

'I believe you could glam her up a bit, make her look nice, if she washes her hair a bit...' – friend

'You sometimes wish she looked a little bit smarter than she's just got up off the sofa' – daughter

Dear Friend

We know your thoughts on clothes: *'How can any sensible person waste their time thinking about clothes when the world is in such crisis?'* Your slightly self-righteous, no-nonsense approach preaches that any woman worth her salt can rely on her brain power and moral virtue. To attract attention by wearing anything vaguely alluring is tantamount to a sin, so you deliberately downplay your looks. You would no more do glamour than go back to un-recycled waste disposal. You are far too responsible and want the world to know this with your premeditated and well thought-out lack of concern with your appearance. Well, to us this smacks of someone who does care about clothes...deeply, but in a way that illustrates your intellectual snobbism. You are, you know, a snob – towards any woman who makes an effort to make herself beautiful.

There is, however, one thing you are forgetting. God and Mother Nature made things beautiful too.

At present, looking attractive makes you feel very uncomfortable and while you look down on air-headed fashion types, you do play a starring role in *Absolutely Fabulous*... as Edina's long-suffering daughter Saffy. Okay, give us the lecture about 'more important things in life', but what is your pig-headed righteousness really hiding? Is it possible that deep down you just don't feel that you're allowed to look lovely? Was your sister always 'the pretty one' and you 'the clever one' or did your parents play the 'it's results that count' drumbeat every time you showed an interest in your looks? This might be why you are unable to accept compliments, always batting off any flattering word with a self-deprecating put-down. And is this why you protect yourself with nondescript clothes that don't provoke opinion one way or the other?

It must be hard for you living in a world so consumed by its manufactured idea of physical perfection. We can understand how the incessant barrage of media calls to be forever sixteen and a size 8 drives you to continue your rebellion against this obsession with looking good. There is, however, a middle way, a way that isn't giving in to media pressure, snide comments or desperate pleas from family and friends. You are a tough nut to crack, but your poverty mentality has told you 'that's too good for you, you don't deserve it' for too long.

We think that it is a good idea for you to start thinking about others. Not the faceless names that decree you are no one if you are fat or badly dressed, but the people who love you. Did you ever consider that by depriving yourself of some decent clothes and a touch of make-up you might be depriving others? It might be that if you have a daughter she is embarrassed by your trucker style. Your friends must long to see you do something to better your appearance, for yourself and for your self-esteem. Dressing 'up' needn't be a self-indulgent exercise. We feel that knowing others will take pleasure in you turning up your pretty dial, might help you find it gratifying to put on clothes that flatter you.

We are not asking you to leap from a cake in a marabou bikini, but we are asking that you start believing that you too can be beautiful. It might also be worth remembering that while your nearest and dearest can see beneath the surface of your 'don't care' veneer, others will find it hard. Your brain can certainly do the talking, but it won't get a chance with new friends because they will run a mile from your Billy Goat Gruff exterior. Be bold, be brave and fight the good fight for a fabulous new – but still worthy and wise – YOU.

Susannah   Trinny
x

The remedy

Clothes are clothes – what's the big deal, we hear you bleat. Well, that is true up to a point...but the cut, colour and fabrics make all the difference.

GETTING BACK IN TOUCH WITH YOUR FEMININITY

Wearing a size XXL T-shirt over baggy jeans, no jewellery and boots gives off a message along the lines of 'I've just parked my truck and I'm off for a few pints and a spot of arm wrestling.' Wearing a fitted T-shirt with a few ropes of beads, a figure-enhancing belt, well-cut jeans and a pair of heels says, 'I'm casual with a twist and ready for anything.'

Get started by standing naked in front of the mirror, cringe-making though this may feel. Really take a good look at your body and notice all your attractive, feminine assets. The first thing you may notice is that, naked, you're in fact two sizes smaller than you seemed in your clothes. Wouldn't you like to dress in a way that will give you a slimmer silhouette but at the same time will disguise any sagginess in the tits, arse and tum?

Which is the narrowest part of your torso? You'll probably find that it's just under your boobs (when they're in a bra). When was the last time that you showed off that bit of your body by wearing a top that is fitted around the ribcage? Do you have lumps and bumps around your tummy? Look for a top that hugs under your boobs and then flares out to cover the bulge.

After their twenties, most women's upper thighs are not the best part of their body, but what about the lower half? Do you have well-turned ankles? Make the most of them in shapely heels. If your upper arms are heavy, wear a three-quarter sleeve that will still show off your slim forearms. Do you have an elegant neck that's hidden by your heavy shirts?

You need to look at your body objectively. Everyone has good parts and bad parts and you must discover yours.

STARTING FROM SCRATCH

You don't need to throw out very much. Your wardrobe is so tragically tiny that there isn't much to cull. It's almost guaranteed that of the little there is, nearly every garment you own covers up all of your body's good points. Donate all those baggy jeans and check shirts to the Bricklayers' Benevolent Society. If you want to change your life it is time to start from scratch.

Begin by putting together a wardrobe of the perfect eight garments: a skirt, trousers, T-shirt, jumper, coat, jacket, dress and shirt that are cut to flatter your body shape. These will give you the building blocks of many different outfits for daytime. Turn to our notebook for more details.

Layering creates a casual, comfortable feel at the same time as flattering your figure.

Compare this to your previous silhouette – you HAVE gone down two sizes.

This zip top is fitted, but the ruching hides any excess tummy rolls.

Suede is THE best fabric for a skirt to hide a middle-age spread, closely followed by corduroy.

These elegant boots are your introduction to heels and shapely legs.

Finishing touches

There are little tricks in a woman's wardrobe that can make a big difference to those eight basic items. For you, this is particularly relevant because you have never accessorised in the past. These are the items that become talking points and talking about girly things will help you to connect with other women.

EYEBROW SHAPERS

A woman's face is framed by her eyebrows. They can be very expressive too; it's possible to communicate so much, from 'Oh, really?' to 'Do you want to come in for coffee?' with just the merest twitch. For years your eyebrows have been growing as wild and free as a hedge of leylandii so the only message you're capable of conveying is 'Where do you keep your strimmer?' You probably haven't got a clue about where to start in creating that suggestive arch, but luckily there are eyebrow shapers available. Just choose the shape you want, stick the template onto your brow and pluck around it. Then define your newly shaped eyebrow by shading with pencil or powder.

HAIR

Get into a haircare routine. After a good haircut at a new hairdresser you need to maintain your hair. So even if it's just once a week, wash and condition your hair, then towel dry it, leave it until nearly dry, then finish with a blow dryer and a metal-based bristle brush which retains the heat, thereby giving your hair a smooth finish.

TINTED LIP BALM

Dry, lined lips age every woman. We know that you're never going to get into that much make-up but a tinted lip balm will do the trick to give your face that little bit of colour. Just keep it in your handbag and apply with a finger regularly. Equally, a sallow complexion can just exaggerate how tired you really are. Take a tiny touch of your lip balm and massage in to the apples of your cheeks.

EYELASH CURLERS

Even if your eyelashes are stubby you can really open up the look of your eyes by curling them. Using a heated eyelash curler makes quick work of it.

SPECTACLES

Now you have achieved those elegant, shapely eyebrows and sweeping lashes, choose a pair of spectacle frames that enhance rather than obliterate them. There are literally thousands to choose from so you will have to take some time and try on many pairs to discover which ones suit the width and shape of your face. Since you last bought spectacles, the shops have developed a system where you can try them on and then photograph yourself to compare later. All the designers are in on the act so you will definitely be able to find a pair that look great on you. Try to think about glasses as facial decoration, rather than medical appliances. Take advantage of those two-for-one offers and kit yourself out with a funky pair for daytime and a more minimal, conservative pair for dinners and dates.

BOOTS

If we had to choose the top five items that we always recommend to every type of woman, these boots would be high up on that list. Whatever your shape, size or weight, these boots suit most women, even if you have chunky calves. Your legs will look longer and you will be able to wear skirt lengths that have never looked good on you before. Your introduction to heels should be in the safest format possible. Although flat looking, these boots actually have a two-and-a-half inch heel but still allow you to feel incredibly stable while attaining a rather more elegant air than your old sturdy boots.

GEL CUSHIONS

There is one positive thing that has come out of the modern mania for plastic surgery. It's the use of silicone gel as a body enhancer – but worn outside of the body. You can get silicone gel enhancers to put in your bra and now silicone gel comfort cushions for your shoes. So wearing stunning high heels to a party need no longer be a form of slow torture.

Life tips

You may have been suffering from a poverty mentality. This is basically a fear that there will not be enough for you in this endless universe. Your thinking bears little relation to your actual circumstances. It is more a deep-down conviction that your life is threatened by financial insecurity and that you must deprive yourself at every opportunity. Try to understand that this mental pattern creates a self-fulfiling prophecy. It's not fair on your friends and family and it's not fair on you, it's just plain mean.

Even if you have very little money, you can still learn to enjoy what you do have rather than fear that you will go without. Make yourself an 'abundance box'. It works like a swear box – every time you hear yourself utter words like 'I can't afford it' or 'The price of lettuce these days' or 'I'm keeping this old sweater for a rainy day' or 'That's too good for me' or any other poverty-inspired statement, put a few coins in the box. In the long term this will help to cure you of deprivation-thinking and then you won't need it anymore. After a couple of months take

all the cash from your abundance box and buy something totally indulgent – cashmere underpants, a top-of-the-range scented candle, a lobster and champagne lunch for one. And come home in a taxi, dammit! You may not use this money for anything useful or practical. Remember, you are giving up the worthy in favour of the frivolous.

Your wardrobe is so tiny it's a crying shame. We mean not only the amount of clothes you own but also your actual cupboards. Size up your home and find some empty corners where you can squeeze in some more hanging space. It may be a nook at the top of the stairs or a few empty feet behind the bedroom door; there is always somewhere. By giving yourself more cupboard space you are also giving yourself permission to own lovely things to put in them. A bit of clever work with a tape measure and an Ikea catalogue will open up your horizons.

As you walk out the door each morning look in the mirror and give yourself a compliment. Write on a postcard 'You look gorgeous', then send it to yourself – it feels so good to receive fan mail.

Take a large piece of paper and write down fifty reasons why you deserve a whole new outfit. As you write, notice which reasons are self-pitying ('I've never had anything nice') and which ones are self-affirming ('I grew the most beautiful peonies in my garden'). Now take a separate piece of paper and write down fifty ways that you could make some extra money to pay for that new outfit. They don't have to be practical, or even sensible. You might think of anything from 'rob a bank' to 'charge a reasonable rate for babysitting my grandchildren'. This is an exercise in firing up your imagination. Just keep writing until you've reached fifty.

Watch films that give you the message that it's okay to be silly and girly sometimes. Settle down for a bumper night in with a tub of strawberry ice cream (or a punnet of strawberries if you're being saintly) and a clutch of videos like *Legally Blonde* and *Bridget Jones's Diary*.

When? An important lunch or daytime occasion, like a christening or garden party.

Why? This outfit is super smart yet relaxed. It looks effortless.

TCR 10:45:58:12 PLAY LOCK

TCR 10:06:27:12 PLAY LOCK

TCR 10:29:19:05 PLAY LOCK

TCR 10:32:53:15 PLAY LOCK

TCR 10:47:39:13 PLAY LOCK

TCR 10:46:03:09 PLAY LOCK

Penni basked in compliments from he

TCR 10:06:33:01
PLAY   LOCK

TCR 10:14:28:21
PLAY   LOCK

TCR 10:41:22:22
PLAY   LOCK

Photo 2

Photo 3
TCR 10:40:36:05
PLAY   LOCK

TCR 10:52:25:02
PLAY   LOCK

TCR 10:56:45:08
PLAY   LOCK

amily and friends. So can you...

Remember

 Put together a capsule wardrobe of the perfect eight items. These will be the building blocks of your new outfits.

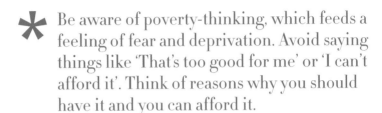 Be aware of poverty-thinking, which feeds a feeling of fear and deprivation. Avoid saying things like 'That's too good for me' or 'I can't afford it'. Think of reasons why you should have it and you can afford it.

Creating more cupboard space also creates a feeling of entitlement. Enjoy filling those shiny new rails.

There is a difference between well fitted and too tight. Wearing clothes that are fitted will make you seem slimmer and shapelier.

Always carry a tinted lip balm in your handbag. Dab it on with a finger to bring your lips and cheeks back to life.

Give yourself a compliment every morning. It might make you laugh, but it will also make you feel good.

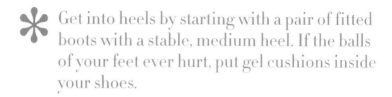 Get into heels by starting with a pair of fitted boots with a stable, medium heel. If the balls of your feet ever hurt, put gel cushions inside your shoes.

 Open up your eyes by shaping your eyebrows and curling your eyelashes.

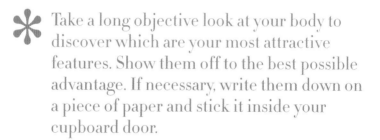 Take a long objective look at your body to discover which are your most attractive features. Show them off to the best possible advantage. If necessary, write them down on a piece of paper and stick it inside your cupboard door.

 Sometimes it's great to be girly. Chick films may seem silly but they're enormous fun to watch. Wearing eye-catching accessories is a great way to strike up casual conversations and connect with other women.

'I can fit in daughter's – and I'm

to my clothes 45!'

'THE CLOTHES MIGHT STILL
FIT BUT DOES YOUR FACE?'

TRINNY AND SUSANNAH

What I say...

I don't want to be that mumsy woman in the corner.

I look as good in my daughter's clothes as she does.

Pretty pastels and frills make me feel girly.

These funky jeans are the latest thing.

I feel younger than all my friends.

I love to go shopping with my daughter.

I'm like a butterfly, flitting around on a cloud.

My hairstyle needs to be fun.

Bright eyeshadow and lipstick cheer me up.

I dress for me, not for *anybody* else.

What I really feel inside...

I dread turning into my mother.

I need to reassure myself that I'm still young and trim.

I'm desperately hanging on to my youth.

I'm running as fast as I can to keep up.

But I'm not.

But my daughter always seems to be 'busy with her friends' on a Saturday.

Sometimes my responsibilities feel like a burden to me.

My hair is fun, but am I?

I worry that my face is ageing and I want to cover it up.

I don't care about anybody else.

How you look

You are walking down the high street, denim-clad butt swaying, pink sparkly clips holding back your sunlit tresses, Mickey Mouse T-shirt, a tiny bit short, displaying your tummy. You hear a wolf whistle. You spin to smile at the owner of the hard, lean, sweat-gleaming torso, who retorts: 'Oops, no, not you, grandma, it's the girl behind you I'm after.'

How humiliating is THAT? The sexy bricky thought you were dead hot until he saw your true age reflected in the wrinkles of your face. This little tale demonstrates perfectly how you look bedecked in your teenage daughter's clothes. The clothes fit your body but not your face.

There is no doubt that being able to fit into your nubile seventeen-year-old daughter's jeans in mid-life is pretty damn cool. The fact that you are the same size is great. But truly, you look ridiculous wearing clothes suitable for lasses on the brink of womanhood. You may feel like a sprightly duckling, but sauntering in Disney-emblazoned merchandise doesn't make you look any younger. It's quite the reverse. Donald Duck does a wonderful job of adding years to you. The little girly accessories are reminiscent of Bette Davis's 'Baby Jane'. The limited edition trainer is fabulous for hip-hopping about your day but more suited to those coming out through the school doors than one of the mums waiting to collect the pupils.

Night-time brings out the 'babe' in you… or so you think. Darkness gives you the opportunity to expose more flesh. You love to pile on the slap. Make-up is a vital fixture of your evening kit. The more you paint on, the more colourful and young you feel. What you fail to see is that the mismatched foundation collects in your laughter lines. You are blind to the garish lipstick bleeding into creases round your mouth. *'The baby blue eye shadow and azure eyeliner makes my blue eyes bluer'*. No, dear girl, they only draw attention to their redness, bloodshot with tiredness from refusing to wear your bi-focals.

It's time to grow up, time to look and act the person your life's experience has made you. A real woman.

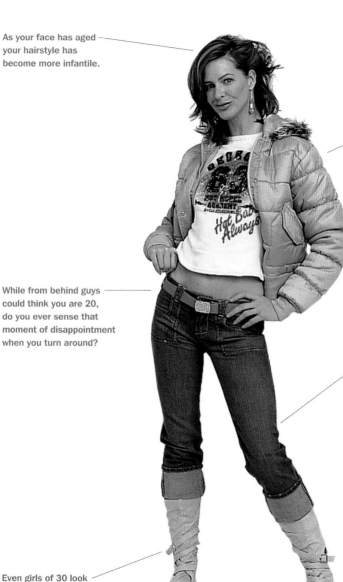

As your face has aged your hairstyle has become more infantile.

Only when you're younger do fun, cheap fashions look funky. On you they just look cheap.

While from behind guys could think you are 20, do you ever sense that moment of disappointment when you turn around?

Teenagers establish their identity by the brand of jeans they wear. Do you still not know who you are?

Even girls of 30 look like mutton in these boots, so what does that really say about a woman of 45?

How others see you

'Too old and a bit mad' – son

'My mum's style is the same as me – and I'm 14!' – daughter

'Maybe it's time to leave all the teenage fashions behind' – best friend

'She wore a short dress with wellies which was – quite funny' – friend's daughter

Dear Friend

Mid-life is a very tough time for women, especially those with teenage daughters who are now getting the attention the mums were once used to. It wasn't so long ago that you were a yummy mummy, all maternal, glowing and Madonna-like. With your toddlers cavorting around your legs, you made a charming picture of a woman in her prime.

Now in the grey light between youth and wisdom you would be so gratefully flattered by the attention of a spotty, sex-obsessed youth that you might take him seriously. We are not saying that a woman isn't attractive in her forties. Far from it. This is when *we* believe a woman is in her prime. It's just that she is even more alluring if she is confident of her age and experience. When a woman doesn't accept that she is getting older she loses all appeal.

It is totally understandable that you want to turn back the clock. For God's sake, what woman doesn't want to re-live her youth. We all have regrets. We all have things we wished we had or hadn't done. We all dream of being twenty-one again and picking up our lives from that age to be all the things we dreamed of but were not experienced enough to become. But as we all know, travelling back in time is impossible, even when wearing the clothes of a woman twenty years your junior.

This, more than any other period in a woman's life, is a time of acceptance. We don't mean you have to give up and give in to old age and we don't dictate a future of blue rinses, floral shirt-waisters and elasticised slacks. A forty-something woman is still young, especially today when it's commonplace to arrive at the Pearly Gates in one's nineties. Flippin' heck, you've still got forty-odd years before you peg it. With this in mind, getting old shouldn't be so scary. It's madness worrying about something that is so far off. Flip this thought process over and look back at the forty-odd years behind you.

They too count for something. Those are decades during which you have evolved. They shouldn't be degraded by trying to be a flighty youngster again.

Next time you find yourself reaching for your daughter's cropped T-shirt and hacking your jeans to make a pair of hot pants, consider her feelings. You can rely on the mother-daughter-isn't-this-fun-to-be-sharing-clothes thing to a certain degree, but maybe she feels you are encroaching on her space and trying to steal her thunder, or she's just plain embarrassed by a mum who refuses to grow up. This could well make her feel insecure or that she is in competition with you. Wouldn't it be great if rather than trying to be her equal, you became her role model, someone who inspires her to get excited about growing up? As you stand, ridiculous in bubble-gum pink and glittery eye shadow, you might well be the butt of her friend's jokes. If this is so, she will be grateful for the change in you, if only to stop having to defend your style to her peers.

We are not for one second saying you have to relinquish your sex appeal, just how you express it. Teenage clothes don't make you sexy, they make you old. Turn your attention to a more adult, subtle way of dressing and you will become genuinely alluring.

The remedy

You are in the enviable position of still having a gorgeous fit figure, so it's not difficult for you to look amazing in clothes. With so much to choose from, you have gone for the childishly obvious way of displaying your body.

CLASSIC YET TRENDY

Growing up does not mean dressing like your mother, your greatest fear. But please allow your daughter to explore her own fashion journey, gaining inspiration from *her* stylish mother. And while you might think that your husband still sees the woman he first met, do you ever consider you might be making *him* feel old?

You are going to create a much more eye-catching and bedazzling look to tempt his eye. This is done by investing in pieces of clothing that are truly stunning and will stand the test of time, that are cut to give you the figure of a goddess, and that leave people with the impression that 'I have innate style and an eye for beauty' rather than 'I'm always running desperately to keep up with the latest fashion'.

COLOURS

We are sure that your wardrobe contains mainly pastels and sparkles. These are just a cry for help in someone your age. With the years, our skin gets paler, which means the blemishes and veins show up more so we have to re-address what really suits us. Play-time bubble-gum colours are for kids. Real women go for drama and sophistication in colour. You should be wearing shades that truly complement your complexion.

SHOPPING FOR QUALITY

You are not in competition with your daughter so stay away from her shops. Teenagers don't have much money, so they buy inexpensive clothes. You have spent the last ten years convincing yourself that you don't spend that much on clothes either because each item is cheap. But if you add up all those little splurges you begin to see the real cost. Get rid of tat to make room for just a few quality items. Plan your new outfit at home and then go out with your list to find the specific item you need to create your new look.

Do not be diverted by anything that shines or sparkles in the corner of your eye. Pay a visit to the top-line designer floor of a leading department store and don't be afraid to try on some fabulous pieces. Even if these are beyond your budget it will give you inspiration and guidance in what to look for. You want to be the perpetual teenager, but why? It is grown women who have all the adventures.

Compare this sleek, sexy style to the fluffy schoolgirl look you used to sport. No contest!

It is possible to dress and still feel the youth and energy that you find lacking in many of your contemporaries, but the difference with this look is that your friends will be coveting the outfit instead of teasingly belittling it.

Replacing your childish emblems with a fun stripy dress and other bold patterns still allows you to maintain a youthful appearance and the figure-hugging shape shows off your well-maintained body.

Wearing a dress over jeans is a great way to keep a young feel. The jeans are now a background to accentuate a good look.

In the past you would have worn boots with your jeans. By wearing an elegant open-toed sandal you create an air of sophistication and quality.

Finishing touches

You have drawers overflowing with belts and jewellery, scarves and handbags. Most of them were picked up from the clearance bins in teen chain stores. While we tell many women that they can update their look with judicious choice of inexpensive accessories, you need to head in the other direction and invest in quality pieces that make a dramatic statement about you as a woman.

QUALITY SHOES

You have dozens of pairs of shoes and boots in your wardrobe. Yet do you own one pair of truly chic shoes? The kind that your daughter would die for, that you would NEVER lend her? Keep them beautifully with shoe trees in their boxes with a Polaroid stuck on the outside for easy identification. Start building your collection now. It is far better to have ten pairs of beautifully kept shoes than forty dusty, scuffed pairs stuffed into the back of your closet.

HAIR

As you have got older your hair has got younger, and the number of hair accessories you wear rivals a Hindu goddess. Unfortunately, on you the effect is that more normally created by a seven year old gone mad with her Sindy doll. Keep your hair simple, shiny and sleek. When you are on holiday you can get away with ONE fabulous silk flower in your hair. For for an evening out or a wedding, try a dramatic jewelled slide or a gorgeous feathered comb. Otherwise avoid all hair accessories. It's about quality, not quantity.

JEWELLERY

Your jewellery box might contain some inherited items you never wear (too matronly!). They are fighting for space with mountains of quick-fix trinkets you grabbed while shopping because they were on special offer by the till. Piled on, they just look cheap. Save your money and go for one amazing statement piece which will make a far greater impact.

JEANS

Your jeans are more embellished than the excuses you use to justify them. On young people, extreme jeans are tribal identification. You can never be a part of their tribe, so you just end up looking like a desperate wannabee. Your jeans should show off to perfection the amazing body you obviously work so hard for. This is done by concentrating on shape and cut rather than decorations and funky logos. Choose jeans that are a classic dark denim. They look more sophisticated and people can focus on your sexy butt.

MAKE-UP

You are still sporting the make-up of your teens, yet your face has lost its first flush of youth. Your make-up palette is way too colourful – all blue eyeshadow and frosty pink lipstick. Your wardrobe has grown up, it's time for your make-up to do the same. Throw out ALL your cosmetics – we are sure that even your mascara is coloured.

Starting afresh you will spend most of your money on really good quality base products, brushes and blusher. You will only need one or two eyeshadows and lip colours.

As we age, the trick is to look like you are wearing less make-up, yet the application requires far more skill. You need to focus more on creating a flawless finish. Pay attention to where age has hit you, the dark circles and spider veins. Cover them with a good concealer coupled with a tinted moisturiser. Use tones that bring out the natural colours of your eyes and lips as opposed to trying to jazz up your face with rainbows of make-up. Go for natural rose lip tones that will reduce ageing. Lastly, a quick lashing of black mascara will enhance your eyes.

RED LIPSTICK

In the evening you need to add some drama to your look. Red lipstick can be stunningly sexy if applied correctly. First apply a wax product, like the Body Shop's Wax Filler, to reduce bleeding. Then, with a rock-steady hand, take a lip pencil in the identical colour to your lipstick to outline the fullest shape of your lips without going outside your natural lip line. Finally, apply the red with a lip brush. For extra staying power, blot your lips and then apply another layer. For a more sexy and less tarty look, use a matt lipstick, rather than gloss.

CHICKEN FILLETS

Although you have taken great care of your body, time has taken its toll on your boobs, unless you have had a boob job. You revert to dressing young because you don't quite know HOW to do sexy. You wear T-shirt bras that give you NO support. What you have to understand is that it is way sexier to look a fabulous forty than a past-it, post-pubescent desperado. Those teenage bras and bikini tops are making your tits look like a pair of cold fried eggs. Get fitted for a bra with more uplift and support. For evenings and special, plunging neckline occasions, fill them out with a pair of silicone gel chicken fillets.

Life tips

You may feel that in some ways your life has passed you by. Not that you don't love being a mother. It's just that one day you looked in the mirror and thought, 'What happened to all my aspirations?' So little by little, you started to live vicariously through your daughter. You want for her all that you dreamed of for yourself. This is no bad thing, but you need to start doing things for your own life, now. She will soon grow up and leave home. Empty-nest syndrome will hit you hard unless you take steps towards fulfilling your own ambitions.

Write a list of your wildest dreams. Be as creative and out-there as possible. Deep-sea diving? No problem. Just keep writing your list and as you write it will become apparent to you which of these are your deepest desires and which are only pipe-dreams. Choose one of them and do something today that will be the first step towards making your ambition a reality. Even if it's only asking for the application form. From now on you are going to take one action every working day (that's five actions a week) towards fulfilling your dream.

Cast your eye about your bedroom. Would Barbie feel more at home in here? Is there any room at all for your husband among all the pastel colours and soft toys? Really think about overhauling the whole interior to create a boudoir that is seductive and grown-up. Rich colours and fabrics are a wonderful setting for night-time encounters.

Go back to school. It really is possible to develop a whole new set of skills in your forties, or beyond. All the major colleges are listed on the internet and will send out free prospectuses. There are adult education institutes galore, offering courses in everything from singing to philosophy. Many universities offer part-time post-graduate courses and you may be eligible through experience alone, without needing to have achieved a degree in the past.

Have you noticed that all the world's most sexy and desirable female icons are not schoolgirls? Cate Blanchett, Nicole Kidman, Julianne Moore, Nigella Lawson. None of these babes could be accused of dressing like mutton or even of trying to deceive about their age. You'd be amazed how many red-blooded men dream about Helen Mirren. Choose a new role model who is roughly your shape and age. Study the way she dresses and carries herself. What is it that makes *her* so seductive?

When? Out dancing with
your husband.

Why? Dressing like a
showstopper will make you
realise that it's real grown
women who attract all the
attention, not little girls.

TCR 10:08:45:20
PLAY   LOCK

TCR 10:01:59:12
PLAY   LOCK

TCR 10:25:33:16
PLAY   LOCK

TCR 10:18:29:16
PLAY   LOCK

TCR 10:23:42:11
PLAY   LOCK

TCR 10:26:38:23
PLAY   LOCK

Judith gained a new level of respect from he

TCR 10:08:43:15 PLAY LOCK

TCR 10:17:32:19 PLAY LOCK

TCR 10:11:36:09 PLAY LOCK

TCR 10:15:59:15 PLAY LOCK

TCR 10:28:45:07 PLAY LOCK

TCR 10:23:31:00 PLAY LOCK

aughter and friends. So can you...

Remember

✳ Learn to investment-dress. Visit the designer floor of a top department store like Selfridges or Harvey Nichols to try on some knock-out garments. See the difference?

✳ It's never too late to fulfil your dreams. Make a start now and take it a day at a time. One action every working day equals five a week, equals twenty per month. You'll soon be there.

✳ When it comes to hair decorations, less is more. De-clutter your hair, keep it sleek and sexy.

✳ Teenage bras have no support so make your tits seem decidedly saggy. Get a bra that lifts and supports, then stuff it full of chicken fillets.

✳ Too-colourful make-up is draining all the life out of your face. Learn new skills in blending a flawless-finish base and using less make-up in subtle hues to bring out your natural skin and eye tones.

Choose a new role model – the Spice Girls are *so over – duh!*

 Specific types of jeans are worn as tribal markers in young people. If you're not one of the gang, then wearing them seems desperate. Choose jeans that tell which tribe you are a part of – the 'I've got a fabulous figure and I'm older than you so I *can* afford them' gang.

 One amazing piece of jewellery makes a big impact and will have all your friends commenting on it.

 Replace those kiddy pastels with sophisticated colour combinations that bring out the woman in you, both in what you wear and in your bedroom.

 Better to have ten pairs of chic shoes than ten times as many scuffed last-year's-hot-look-now-slightly-out-of-date pairs.

'This has always
been my b

ways
est look'

'THAT WAS 20 YEARS AGO'

TRINNY AND SUSANNAH

What I say...

I have some fabulous clothes that I bought when I was younger.

In my head I'm still slim and thirty.

I'm divorced, but I still wear my wedding ring on a chain round my neck.

Longer skirts make me feel older.

I have so many old photographs, I can't throw a single one away.

I don't believe that new underwear, new clothes and a new hairstyle could make a difference to how I feel inside.

These shoes match my handbag.

This outfit reminds me of my son's christening.

But this look has always suited me!

What I really feel inside...

My best times are in the past.

But in reality I'm a decade or two older and a size or two bigger.

Sometimes it feels like a millstone round my neck, yet somehow I'm not quite ready to break free.

But then so does showing my saggy knees.

I find letting go of the past really painful.

I'm afraid to lose my identity.

I don't know how else to accessorise.

I don't want him to grow up and move away.

Denial is so very comfortable.

How you look

Dated is the first word that springs to mind when meeting you. Old fashioned, garish and fake describes your style. We could say: clothes by *Dallas* and *Dynasty*, hair by *Charlie's Angels*, accessories by Margaret Thatcher after a shopping binge in Ratner's. Your moments of glory were between your twenties and thirties and you have resolutely clung to the time you felt and looked your best.

The reason you appear old hat is because you have clung to a series of signature styles belonging to two past decades. It is immediately possible to date your power shoulder-padded jacket and the golden chains that adorn your neck and handbags to the eighties. Your feather-cut mullet screams glam rock and roll 1970s. You are very definitely of a certain age. Around the same age as us, actually, or a little older.

Casting our minds back over time in terms of fashion, the two (in our opinion) most ghastly decades were the seventies and eighties. When we see pictures of ourselves with big hair, big pearls, big sodding awful everything, we die of embarrassment. In fact, nearly every woman we know does the same. Extraordinary, then, that you should still be dressing in a way that hasn't moved on...AT ALL.

Much of what you wear will have been in your closet since your heyday. Some of the pieces will have been expensive. They will be well made. Well, of course everything was in those days, wasn't it? That's your excuse. Your husband loved this one and that one. You got your job in this suit and christened your son in that dress. Your wardrobe is wall-to-wall memories.

You are wearing your past, not clothes to flatter who you have become over the years. For goodness sake, it has to be time to get away from thick-denier flesh-coloured tights, chunky gold and pearl costume jewellery, and sky blue skirt suits. Do you really want to look like Ivana Trump at her worst? Forever? We think not.

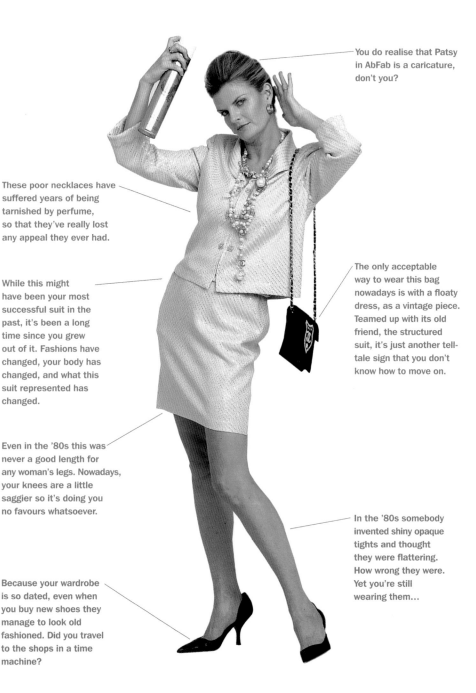

You do realise that Patsy in AbFab is a caricature, don't you?

These poor necklaces have suffered years of being tarnished by perfume, so that they've really lost any appeal they ever had.

While this might have been your most successful suit in the past, it's been a long time since you grew out of it. Fashions have changed, your body has changed, and what this suit represented has changed.

Even in the '80s this was never a good length for any woman's legs. Nowadays, your knees are a little saggier so it's doing you no favours whatsoever.

Because your wardrobe is so dated, even when you buy new shoes they manage to look old fashioned. Did you travel to the shops in a time machine?

The only acceptable way to wear this bag nowadays is with a floaty dress, as a vintage piece. Teamed up with its old friend, the structured suit, it's just another tell-tale sign that you don't know how to move on.

In the '80s somebody invented shiny opaque tights and thought they were flattering. How wrong they were. Yet you're still wearing them…

How others see you

'I don't think she follows trends, she *reads* magazines – but she doesn't take any notice' – student

'She's stuck in the twentieth century' – son

'I've tried so hard to get her out of her short skirts and short tops, and everything has to match' – daughter

'She looks old and fat' – son

'Her hair is a bit '70s, or '80s-ish, reminiscent of Kevin Keegan in his Liverpool days' – student

Dear Friend

You remember as clear as Crystal Carrington the days when you ruled the world...well, your world. You were queen bee of all you surveyed. Popular, inspirational, centre of attention. In charge. In control. The heady days when life was exciting, rewarding and fulfilling. Thank goodness for your memory, huh! Without that, you wouldn't so successfully be living in a time warp. You wouldn't be comfortable walking around as though fresh from the set of Southfork. You wouldn't be at ease in the knowledge that fashion has moved on through so many cycles that your style, complete with shoulder pads and bouffant hair, has rendered you well and truly past your sell-by date.

We have to tell you that your head is buried so deeply in the sands of time and is so heavy with hairspray that you are unable to lift it to see the world as it is today. The strange thing is that all those around you have moved on and gradually you have fallen out of your depth. Maybe your marriage disintegrated or your fabulous job failed to realise your expectations. As a result you take comfort in looking at yourself as you were twenty years ago.

It is obvious to see by your clothes that you are stuck sartorially. Invariably this will mean you are mentally stuck as well. The fact that you were blinkered to the passing of decades in fashion suggests that there may be other areas crying out for re-evaluation. This comfortable rut has been created as a haven. It's not that you don't like clothes, nor do you have a fear of spending money on them. In fact, you truly appreciate a beautifully tailored garment... just as long as it protects you on the front line of emotional breakdown. Interesting, because everyone sees you as a strong woman. Someone who has survived a lot and come out the other side still standing, albeit in a pair of stiletto court shoes.

But how much did those setbacks really affect you? Have you been honest with your friends? Have you indeed been honest with yourself? Are you scared to walk away from your heyday because if you do, life's knocks will reduce you to rubble? Are your armour-plated outfits actually holding together someone as fragile as a cracked windscreen? It's a shame that it's the clothes rather than the emotions of your bygone years that have stuck with you.

You need to delve deep into what made you such a force in the seventies and eighties. That core strength will still be there, it's just been sat on by growing insecurity and fear of change. By changing your look you will open yourself up to new experiences and reactions from others. They probably assume that you are just fine in your drag queen persona. After all, the most successful transvestites assume the eighties power dressing look, possibly because it is the most masculine fashion this side of the 1930s. Clothes can do an awful lot to help a woman move on, but they can also act as a prison. You decide what yours have been doing to your life.

Susannah   Trinny
x

The remedy

It will be difficult to let go of your emotional attachment to a look that you have worn for the last *twenty years* (think about that), nevertheless it's well past its sell-by date. Some of your beloved relics have to go to a better place, but others can be resurrected and join the contemporary world.

HOW TO WEAR SEPARATES

The most certain way to look stuck in the past is to wear everything matching: shoes and bag, necklace and earrings, jacket and trousers. In your mind, wearing a suit has always equalled looking smart. Re-educate yourself on ways to dress in different situations. You can still wear your jackets, but not with their matching skirts. Team them instead with a pair of jeans and fitted T-shirt for a relaxed lunch, or a pretty patterned skirt for a smarter occasion.

When buying skirts and tops choose modern colours that are a shade or two away from each other, rather than matching. If you're top heavy, wear the darker shade on your top half. If your bum and thighs are big, cover them with the darker colour. Learn to buy clothes that show off your figure to its best advantage.

Try on tops that skim, rather than cling. Look at your fabrics too. Many modern fibres are much more flattering to the body so clothes need not be so structured and rigid as in the past. Try trousers cut on the hip, sheer lightweight jerseys that are draped or ruched to disguise unwanted bumps.

ALTERATIONS

With a bit of smart seamstressing your quality garments can be reborn into the 21st century. Remove all shoulder pads – this will immediately soften your look. Move the buttons to make a jacket more fitted. Jackets can be nipped in at the waist with a simple back seam alteration. Replace any gilt buttons, they're a dead giveaway as to the era of the jacket. All high-waisted and front-pleated trousers or – God forbid! – stirrup pants just have to be got rid of. They make any woman look like she's swallowed a basketball. Most of your skirts will have to go too. If any of your skirts *can* be let down to the knee, then it is worth having those too-tight waistbands replaced with a simple binding. A skirt sitting on the hip is far more flattering than a waistband clamping your middle and pushing out folds of flab. Look at our notebook for chapter 4 for tips on finding a dressmaker.

This hairstyle is smart and finished but so much more approachable than your old lacquered-to-within-an-inch-of-its-life look. A passing man might even want to run his fingers through it.

Huge earrings bring all the attention to your face. These stand out on their own without the need for a matching necklace.

This top seems casual, yet worn with the skirt the overall effect is stunning. Playing it down in fabulous colours and shapes is far more effective than getting done up like the old dog's dinner.

If you have an hourglass figure: this skirt is a very good way to show it off. It ends at the perfect place, just on the knee, to elongate your legs. The last thing it looks is frumpy.

These tights are sheer and sexy, giving the best possible shape to your legs.

It's chic to wear shoes that coordinate with the colour of your outfit, rather than match it.

Finishing touches

There's no point in modernising your clothes if you insist on continuing to accessorise them in such a dated way.

UNDERWEAR

You probably have no idea about the amazing new developments in underwear. We're not talking about sexy, pretty lingerie. We're talking about technology that takes off 10 pounds. This is all the armour your body needs to get away with the sheer, fitted styles we are suggesting. Magic knickers smooth any lumps and bumps while holding in your saddlebags and lifting up your bum. The longline style that Susannah is wearing below flattens the tummy, allowing not an inch of overspill.

For more laid-back occasions, try a pair of Brazilian bum-lift tights. For the extra special silk dress moment, Rigby & Peller make an elasticated full body corset that will give you the freedom to wear that slinky number without feeling self conscious about your figure. Get yourself kitted out with clever underwear before you go shopping for clothes.

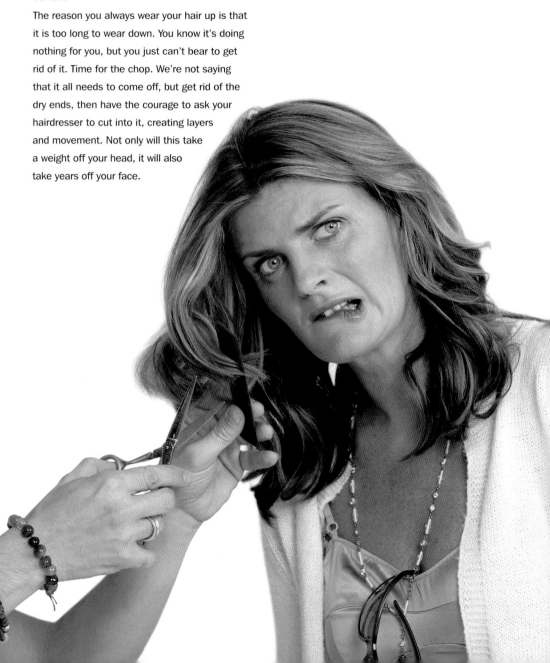

HAIR

The reason you always wear your hair up is that it is too long to wear down. You know it's doing nothing for you, but you just can't bear to get rid of it. Time for the chop. We're not saying that it all needs to come off, but get rid of the dry ends, then have the courage to ask your hairdresser to cut into it, creating layers and movement. Not only will this take a weight off your head, it will also take years off your face.

JEWELLERY

If you have any earrings in your jewellery box
that resemble the gilt buttons on your old suits,
get rid of them. You need to travel from one
extreme to the other. The old *Dynasty* style
earrings are so severe. Ethnic jewellery is much
more feminine and relaxed, yet it still attracts
the eye. Look for earrings that pick out one
or two of the colours in your outfit rather than
matching with the clasp on your handbag.

In general, the modern way to wear jewellery
is much more eclectic than in the past. It's all
about pick and mix rather than wearing a set.
Some simple rules: you can wear
any amount of necklaces or
earrings as wild as you like,
but never both at the same
time; avoid mixing metals;
don't overdo the diamanté.
More is sometimes more
– if you find a great
bracelet in a high street
shop, buy three or four
and wear them
all together.

NAIL VARNISH

Those outmoded oranges and pinks are stuck
to your nails like barnacles. Just get rid of all
the nail varnish you own and replace it. For your
everyday look, go for clean, buffed nails with
just a bit of clear gloss to give them a healthy
sheen. For a more glamorous
look, choose a modern colour,
like dark burgundy, but make
sure that your nails are not
too long, otherwise you'll
just look vampish.

CLINIQUE
glosswear
nail enamel

HANDBAGS

You're a bit of a handbag collector, you feel no need to throw them away because you think they're timeless. Bags are only timeless if they started out in life as classics and have been preserved and maintained really well. If they're a bit scuffed or dusty, they just don't look great anymore. That tired navy leather handbag with the gold clasp is completely dating your whole look. Your good-quality 1980s handbag probably cost you £50, and that was a lot of money in those days, so you still drag it out at every occasion.

Do you realise that now you can buy fabulous handbags for less than £25, in today's money? There are quite a few high street shops with a wide range of the prettiest handbags that are softer, more modern than the ones you're used to. A soft handbag in suede, fabric or corduroy gives a much more casual feel and will help to update some of those dresses which you have removed the shoulder pads from. You may be able to adapt some of your structured handbags by removing the straps, then using the bags as clutch bags.

MAKE-UP

Again, those matt, one-colour orange or pink lipsticks went out with the ark, but they're still lurking in your bathroom cabinet, along with the industrial-strength foundation and loose powder that together could double as a wall filler. Topped off with a bronzy powder blusher you look like you are trying to resurrect the whole cast of *Dallas*. Start with some lightweight moisturising foundation the same colour as your skin (this is one area where matching is a *good* thing). Blend a little cream blusher onto the apples of your cheeks rather than in the hollow under the cheekbone. Now finish with a subtle lip gloss.

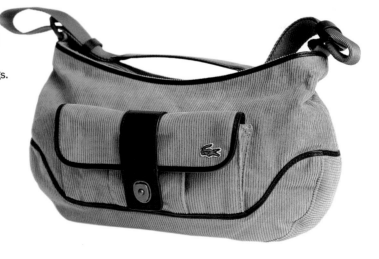

Life tips

Staying stuck in the past has allowed others to pigeon-hole you for far too long. It's time to show the world your true potential.

Take the next step up in your career. Now that you've reinvented your look, others will be looking at you differently. So strike while the iron is hot. Just feel the fear and apply for that promotion, an entirely new job or even go back to college. The new you can do it. The only way now is forward.

Along with shoulder pads, smoking went out in the eighties. Let the ciggies go and you may well find that all sorts of other habits that trapped you in your past go with them. This is a very difficult and courageous thing to do. Just remember that it's a new adventure every day and if you don't keep going you'll never find out where the journey is taking you. A tip – get rid of all your smoking-related paraphernalia. Those souvenir ashtrays,

matchbooks from glamorous restaurants, pearl-inlaid lighters and silver matchbox holders have got to go. No matter how much you loved them, they are a part of your past.

Allow yourself a scruffy day. Spend twenty-four hours wearing a non-structured, non-fitted, non-matching outfit. The very idea may give you the horrors but it will be liberating.

Create a continuous awareness of your life by keeping a journal. Sit down at the end of each day and just write for ten minutes. No more, no less. What did you do today? How did you feel? After a while you may begin to see the old patterns of behaviour and thinking that are keeping you stuck. What small thing could you do differently today to change them? Living in today allows endless possibilities for your future.

Revitalise your diet. You've probably got into the habit of cooking the same meals, using the same ingredients on a weekly basis. According to Dr Gillian McKeith, you can increase your energy by eating plenty of sprouts (such as mung bean sprouts or alfalfa sprouts) and seeds (like pumpkin and sunflower). Try adding them to salads, they are delicious. For an instant pick-me-up, get down to your nearest health food shop and order a shot of wheatgrass juice – with an orange juice chaser. Wheatgrass tastes absolutely vile but really gives you an energy boost.

When? A meeting with your boss – to ask for a promotion!

Why? This modern smart casual look shows that you are moving forward with style and confidence.

TCR 10:01:52:03 PLAY LOCK

TCR 10:01:08:05 PLAY LOCK

TCR 10:04:38:07 PLAY LOCK

TCR 10:12:10:12 PLAY LOCK

TCR 10:17:29:02 PLAY LOCK

TCR 10:22:32:20 PLAY LOCK

Sandie let go of her past and stepped int

TCR 10:07:07:19
PLAY   LOCK

TCR 10:06:45:02
PLAY   LOCK

TCR 10:19:04:06
PLAY   LOCK

TCR 10:16:54:08
PLAY   LOCK

TCR 10:24:23:14
PLAY   LOCK

TCR 10:24:01:02
PLAY   LOCK

oday looking fabulous. So can you...

Remember

* Don't be pigeon-holed at work any longer. Apply for a pay rise, a new position, or even a new job.

* Find a great seamstress who can revitalise all those old jackets. Lose the shoulder pads and replace any dated buttons. Nip in the waists, then wear the jackets as separates with new skirts or jeans.

* Smoking, like *Dallas*, is a thing of the past. Give it up, along with all your souvenir ashtrays and your favourite mother-of pearl lighter.

* Get your hair cut and add movement with layers. It will lighten up your face.

* Be more eclectic with accessories. Matching just makes you look dated. Look for shoes and handbags that come from the same style family, but avoid same colour, same fabric, same decoration.

Keep a journal of your thoughts and actions.
Living in today will open new doors to the future.

Loosen up your look. Learn to wear separates
and colours that coordinate but don't match.
Update the colour palette of your wardrobe by
adding some modern tops and scarves.

Add sprouts and seeds to your salads to help
build up your energy levels. Vary your diet to
include lots of fish and green vegetables.

Shiny or opaque tights are very dating.
Get yourself some sheer natural tights and lots
of fishnets in colours to complement your
clothes. They're the most flattering for any
leg shape. Slim legs can wear a large gauge
fishnet, chunky legs need a finer mesh.

Modern underwear has gone through a technological
revolution. Go shopping for clever foundation
garments before you buy any new clothes.

Trinny & Susannah's notebook of useful information

We get so many letters from our readers asking where we buy our clothes. While individual items are constantly changing from season to season, and even week to week, our notebook lets you know where we usually buy all the clothes that we wear ourselves and recommend to women on our television shows and which shops are most useful to check out to create your own versions of our looks.

1 WHAT'S THE *POINT* IN MAKING AN EFFORT ANYMORE?   10

The remedy   20
Coat by Laura Ashley – 0871 230 2301
Trousers by Zara – 020 7534 9500

Finishing touches   22
Scarf by Etro – 020 7495 5767
Sandals by Topshop – 0800 731 8284
Handbag by Zara – 020 7534 9500
Earrings by Erickson Beamon – 020 7259 0202
Vita-C Max A Perfect One Minute Facial by Jason – 020 7435 5911
Clear make-up bag by Marks & Spencer – 0845 302 1234

Make-up bag contains:
Ultra-C Eye Lift by Jason – 020 7435 5911
Kiss Me lip gloss by Philosophy – 0870 990 8452
Powder blush by Bourjois – 0800 269 836
Concealer by Barbara Daly for Tesco – 0800 505 555
Great Lash mascara by Maybelline – www.maybelline.co.uk
Light-effect concealer pen by Barbara Daly for Tesco – 0800 505 555
Nail varnish by Clinique – 01730 232 566

Life tips   26
Dress by Allessandra DellAcqua, available at Selfridges – 0870 837 7377
Shoes by Gina – 020 7409 7090
Earrings by Erickson Beamon – 020 7259 0202

A great book for you:
The Artist's Way by Julia Cameron, published by Pan Books

2 I HAVE AN IMAGE TO UPHOLD   32

The remedy   42
Suit by Amanda Wakeley – 020 7590 9105 www.amandawakeley.com
T-shirt by Jigsaw – 020 7491 4484

Finishing touches   44
Sandals by Prada – 020 7647 5000
Necklace by Principles – 0870 122 8802
Hairclip by Accessorize – 0870 412 9000 www.accessorize.co.uk
Handbag by Hermès – 020 7499 8856

Handbag contains:
Heels by Jimmy Choo – 020 7584 6111
Earrings by Erickson Beamon – 020 7259 0202

Society in England, 50 Gloucester Place,
London W1 – 020 7935 9261
www.dhyanacentre.org or www.theoseoc.org.uk.
To find a class outside London try entering
'meditation class' + uk into your search engine.
There are many to choose from.

Cardigan by Jigsaw – 020 7491 4484
Skirt by Zara – 020 7534 9500
*Avoid the frumpy second floor of the department store,
instead head for high-street shops like Jigsaw,
Principles and Monsoon. As well as catering for up
to size 16 (Jigsaw), 18 (Monsoon) and 20
(Principles), they understand how to cut clothes to
suit a woman's shape rather than just trying to force her
into the latest fashions.*

Follow our jeans shape guide below to find
the style that will enhance your figure.

Your figure	Style to wears
Hour glass	A slim-leg boot cut style will balance out your hips and shoulders.
Wider thighs, pert bottom	Shaded denim jeans which are lighter on the front of the thighs and darker on the sides will give a slimming effect to your legs.
No bum	Flap pockets on the bottom create the illusion of a shapely butt.
Short legs, pear shaped	Wear long legged, wide leg jeans over heels or wedges to maximise the length of your legs.
Big bottom, slim thighs	A low-rise wide-leg or boot-cut style will make your bottom look smaller.
Big bottom, big thighs	Go for wide-leg trousers in a fine denim (also called chambray). Heavy weight denim jeans are too thick and too clingy for your body shape. They will only make your bum and thighs look larger.

Stockists for jeans:
Gap – 0800 731 8284
H&M – 020 7323 2211
Topshop – 0845 121 4519
Dorothy Perkins – 0845 121 4515
Warehouse – 0870 122 8813
River Island – 020 8991 4759
Levis – 01604 599 752
James, available at Selfridges – 0870 837 7377

7 For all Mankind, available at Joseph –
  020 7823 9500
Chloé – 020 7823 5348
Evisu – 020 7292 0500
Earl Jeans – 020 7727 9902
Joes Jeans, available at Harvey Nichols –
  020 7235 5000
Lee – 0845 600 8383
Full Circle – 020 8753 0384
575 Denim available at Selfridges – 0870 837 7377
Calvin Klein Jeans, available at Selfridges –
  0870 837 7377
Replay – 020 7713 9404
Gas – 020 7354 2784
Diesel – 020 7833 2255

Fishnets by Jonathan Aston at Mytights.com –
  www.mytights.com
Sandals by Prada – 020 7647 5000
Earrings by Accessorize – 0870 412 9000
  www.accessorize.co.uk
Bag by Per Una at Marks & Spencer – 0845 302 1234
Mostro trainers by Puma – 01924 425 555
Pout Plump by Pout 020 7379 0379 www.pout.co.uk
Pinch Your Cheeks stain applied to lips with **retractable
lip brush**, both by Origins – 0800 731 4039

Trousers by Goat, available at Harvey Nichols –
  020 7235 5000
Shirt by Joseph – 020 7823 9500
Shrug by River Island – 020 8991 4759
Brooch by Erickson Beamon – 020 7259 0202
Shoes by LK Bennett – 020 7491 3005

Top by Zara – 020 7534 9500
Jeans by Chloé – 020 7823 5348
Vintage fake fur coat from Rellik – 020 8962 0089
How to buy vintage:
Top of the line are all the major auction houses, which
  hold fashion sales regularly. Become a subscriber
  so that you can receive the catalogues in advance.
Specialist stores – They do all the hard work for you.
  You will still have to rummage, but the more
  expensive the garment is the more beautifully they
  will have restored it to its former glory.
Vintage fairs – Usually held in town halls or similar
  venues, this is where all the vintage dealers get
  together so there's a great selection in one place
  and prices are competitive. You can bargain.
Charity stores – These days many of the big charity

stores employ specialists who siphon off all the best stuff and sell it straight on to the dealers so treasures are harder and harder to find. Look for charity shops in out of the way places.

Car boot sales – There are gems to be found if you're knowledgeable and dedicated enough to trawl through acres of junk.

eBay – www.ebay.co.uk

If you're too busy or just plain technophobic there are now services that will handle eBay sales for you. Auctioning4u will value, photograph and handle your sale, in return for a third of the money!
–www.auctioning4u.co.uk

There is a huge amount of information about volunteering available from Volunteering England, including your local volunteer bureau, ideas about what you could do and information on employee volunteering – www.volunteering.org.uk

Debtors Anonymous holds regular meetings which are free and open to anyone who thinks they may have a problem with debt – for information about UK and Ireland meetings contact 020 7644 5070 www.debtorsanonymous.info. There are online groups operating through the USA based website www.debtorsanonymous.org

Debt advice fact sheets from the Citizens Advice Bureaux are available at www.adviceguide.org.uk

Two great books for you:

How to Get What You Want and Want What You Have by John Gray, published by Vermilion

How to Get Out of Debt, Stay Out of Debt and Live Prosperously by Jerrold Mundis, published by Bantam Books

The perfect 8, a capsule wardrobe that will give you the building blocks of your outfits for daytime:

The skirt	Plain corduroy or suede are flattering and versatile for daytime
The trousers	Low waisted, cord or wool
The T-shirt	A flattering shape in white and two of your best colours
The jumper	In the same two best colours, but a tone lighter or darker than your two T-shirts so they look great when layered together
The jacket	FITTED at the waist in denim (the only place we want you to wear it) or corduroy
The coat	If you're only going to have one coat, make it good-quality wool, fitted and brown, not black
The dress	The most practical dress, which suits most women's body shape, is the jersey wrap. Every high-street chain does a version
The shirt	It has to be fitted. Men's shirts do not suit women, except in bed

To discover the best cut for your particular body shape refer back to our original book What Not to Wear – the Rules.

Two great books for you:
Earn What You Deserve by Jerrold Mundis, published by Bantam Books
First Impressions by Ann Demarais and Valerie White, published by Hodder Mobius

Dress by Warehouse – 0870 122 8813
Top by Amanda Wakeley – 020 7590 9105 www.amanadawakeley.co.uk
Jeans by For All Mankind – available at Harvey Nichols 020 7235 5000
Sophisticated looks at affordable prices can be had from the Designers at Debenhams range – 020 7408 4444 www.debenhams.com

Necklace by Erickson Beamon – 020 7259 0202
Sandals by Jimmy Choo – 020 7584 6111
Gel bra inserts from Marks & Spencer – 0845 302 1234
Lip Glaze in plum by Stila – 01730 232 566
Lipstick in Tango Red by Laura Mercier – available at SpaceNK 020 8740 2085
Future Skin oil-free gel foundation by Chantecaille – available at Fenwick 020 7629 9161

Trousers by Joseph – 020 7823 9500
Bustier by Prada – 020 7647 5000
Earrings by Erickson Beamon – 020 7259 0202
Heels by Gina – 020 7235 2932 www.ginashoes.com
Bust by Wonderbra – 0500 362 430
The Open University – www.open.ac.uk

Top by Nougat, available at House of Fraser – 020 7963 2000
Skirt by Stella McCartney – 020 7518 3100
Shoes by Miu-Miu – 020 7409 0900

Magic Knickers by Spanx at Mytights.com – www.mytights.com
Earrings by Butler and Wilson
Toenails painted with **Clinique glosswear nail enamel**

in crushed velvet – 01730 232 566
Handbag by Lacoste – 020 7439 2213

Top by Marni, available at Selfridges – 0870 837 7377 www.selfridges.co.uk
Shoes by Topshop – 0845 121 4519
Trousers by Joseph – 020 7823 9500
Cardigan by Goat, available at Harvey Nichols – 020 7235 5000
Bag by Follie Follie – 020 7287 9912
Vintage necklace from Camden Market
Sunglasses by Giorgio Armani – 01423 520 303
Smoking quitline – 0800 169 0169
Two great books for you:
Feel the Fear and Do It Anyway by Susan Jeffers, published by Arrow Books
You Are What You Eat by Dr Gillian McKeith, published by Michael Joseph

ON THE COVER

Susannah wears
T-shirt by Zara – 020 7534 9500
Face and body foundation by Mac – 020 7534 9222
Colourless face powder by Shu Uemera – 020 7420 7635
Eyebrow duo by Laura Mercier, available at SpaceNK – 020 8740 2085
Powder blush in Tenderling by Mac – 020 7534 9222
Lip glaze in Brown Sugar by Stila – 01730 232 566
Eyeshadows in Columbia and Caramel by Cargo, available at Pout – 020 7379 0379
Pure Colour eyeshadow in Teabox by Estée Lauder – 01730 232 566
False Lash Effect mascara by YSL – 01444 255 700

Trinny wears
T-shirt by Jean Paul Gaultier, available at Selfridges – 0870 837 7377 www.selfridges.co.uk
Breastplate by Prada – 020 7647 5000
Face and body foundation by Mac – 020 7534 9222
Colourless face powder by Shu Uemera – 020 7420 7635
Eyebrow duo by Laura Mercier, available at SpaceNK – 020 8740 2085
Rouge pots blusher in Water Lily by Stila – 01730 232 566
Lip gloss in Blush Shine by Stila – 01730 232 566
Eyeshadow in Starlight by Stila – 01730 232 566
Pure Colour eyeshadow in Teabox by Estée Lauder – 01730 232 566
Eyeshadow trio in Banana Daquiri by Stila – 01730 232 566
False Lash Effect mascara by YSL – 01444 255 700

Susan and Jinny Editing

David Design and art direction

Domenic, Daren and Jason Design

Robin and Aitken Photography

Charlotte Make-up

Cristiano and Henry Hair

Mario Colour

Jessica For continuing to work with us

Zoe Styling and putting up with us

Oriana and Liberty Patience

Caroline and Leanda Organisation

Antonia and Jacinta Dealing with clothing chaos

Tracy, Vicki and all at WNTW

Our families For continued support and love

Jenny and E.J. Bringing up babies

Danielle Hand holding

Claire, Helle, Judith, Lisa, Lyn, Lynda,
Michalina, Penni, Sandie, Sara, Tracy
and all the women who have contributed to
What Not to Wear